How to Care for a Cancer

Real Life Guidance on How to Get Along and Be Friends with the 4th Sign of the Zodiac

T0159458

How to Care
for a Cancer

Real Life Guidance on How
to Get Along and Be Friends with
the 4th Sign of the Zodiac

Mary English

Winchester, UK
Washington, USA

First published by Dodona Books, 2013
Dodona Books is an imprint of John Hunt Publishing Ltd., Laurel House, Station Approach,
Alresford, Hants, SO24 9JH, UK
office1@jhpbooks.net
www.johnhuntpublishing.com
www.dodona-books.com

For distributor details and how to order please visit the 'Ordering' section on our website.

Text copyright: Mary English 2013

ISBN: 978 1 78279 063 1

A CIP catalogue record for this book is available from the British Library.

Design: Lee Nash

Printed and bound by CPI Group (UK) Ltd, Croydon, CR0 4YY

We operate a distinctive and ethical publishing philosophy in all
areas of our business, from our global network of authors to
production and worldwide distribution.

CONTENTS

Also by Mary English

6 Easy Steps in Astrology
The Birth Charts of Indigo Children
How to Survive a Pisces (O-Books)
How to Bond with an Aquarius (O-Books)
How to Cheer Up a Capricorn (O-Books)
How to Believe in a Sagittarius (O-Books)
How to Win the Trust of a Scorpio (Dodona Books)
How to Love a Libra (Dodona Books)
How to Soothe a Virgo (Dodona Books)
How to Lavish a Leo (Dodona Books)
How to Listen to a Gemini (Dodona Books)
How to Satisfy a Taurus (Dodona Books)
How to Appreciate an Aries (Dodona Books)

This book is dedicated to Astrologer Donna Cunningham as without her wise counsel this series of books would never have been born.

Acknowledgements

I would like to thank the following people:

My son for being the Libran that makes me always look on the other side.

My Taurus husband Jonathan for being the most wonderful man in my world.

Mabel, Jessica and Usha for their Homeopathic help and understanding.

Laura and Mandy for their friendship.

Judy Hall for her inspiration.

Alois Treindl for being the Pisces that founded the wonderful Astro.com website.

Judy Ramsell Howard at the Bach Centre for her encouragement.

John my publisher for being the person that fought tooth and nail to get this book published and all the staff at O-Books including Lee, Nick, Trevor, Kate, Catherine, Elizabeth, Maria and Mary.

Mary, Oksana, Fiona, Denise, Octinur and Jacqueline for their welcome editing eyes.

And last but not least my lovely clients for their valued contributions.

Introduction

The more we care for the happiness of others, the greater our own sense of well-being becomes.
Dalai Lama

Why the title of this book? I didn't set out to write a whole series of Astrology books. I started with just one, about my own sign Pisces and I titled it *How to Survive a Pisces* as an instruction manual to help people understand my sign. And when my publisher accepted the book for publication, he took it on one condition, that I didn't write just one book. It was then that I realised I'd got rather a long project on my hands! When I finished Pisces, my clients, friends and family all wanted to know when I was going to write about *their* sign. As I'd started at the last sign of the Zodiac, I thought I'd go backwards through the signs, in typical Pisces fashion, so here I am at Cancer, the sign of the crab.

The title of this book is designed to help you understand and care for the Cancer in your life. You might even be one yourself, or you've given birth to one, or you're dating one, related to one, or you are friends with one.

Millions of people every day read their stars for all kinds of different reasons. Some people want to know, briefly, what's going to happen in the next 24 hours. Some are just curious and others read their stars for guidance or inspiration, or when they're feeling low as a little pick-me-up.

In a YouGov survey of 2,090 Great Britain adults in 2010 it was revealed that only 2% of participants *didn't* know what star sign they were.[1] This means a massive 98% did.

And where, you wonder, did they get this information from? The top three sources of data were from newspapers, magazines and the Internet. But newspaper astrological columns only started in 1930, so people born before this date (my mother being one of them) are unlikely to know what sign they are, as they weren't brought up having this information freely available.

However, Astrology was born a long, long time before 1930 and originated in Babylon over 3,000 years ago.

Christopher McIntosh, a historian, tells us in his *The Astrologers and Their Creed*:

The priests of this kingdom made the discovery, which developed into what we now call astronomy and the zodiacal system of the planets, which we call astrology today. For many generations they painstakingly recorded the movements of these heavenly bodies. Eventually, they discovered, by careful calculation, that in addition to the Sun and the Moon, five other visible planets moved in specific directions every day. These were the planets that we now call Mercury, Venus, Mars, Jupiter and Saturn.

The priests lived highly secluded lives in monasteries adjacent to massive pyramidal observation towers called ziqqurats. Every day they observed the movements of the planets and noted down any corresponding earthly phenomena from floods to rebellions. They came to the conclusion that the laws which governed the movements of the stars and planets also governed events on Earth.

In the beginning the stars and planets were regarded as being actual gods. Later, as religion became more sophisticated, the two ideas were separated and the belief developed that the god 'ruled' the corresponding planet.

Gradually, a highly complex system was built up in which each planet had a particular set of properties ascribed to it. This system was developed partly through the reports of the priests and partly through the natural characteristics of the planets. Mars was seen to be red in colour and was therefore identified with the god Nergal, the fiery god of war and destruction.

Venus, identified by the Sumerians as their goddess Inanna, was the most prominent in the morning, giving birth, as it were, to the day. She therefore became the planet associated with the female qualities of love, gentleness and reproduction.[2]

Eventually astrology made its way across the oceans to Greece, Egypt, Rome in Italy and then to the rest of Europe, changing little in meaning and delivery in that time. Early astrologers had to be able to read and write and calculate difficult mathematical placements of the planets, something that computers now do easily. You won't have to do anything difficult to make the birth charts we're going to make in this book.

I'd like to make a few distinctions about what Astrology is, and isn't. A lot of people seem to think that Astrology is all about prediction. As if all Astrologers do all day is look 'into the future'. This is not entirely true. There are all sorts of Astrologers, just as there are all sorts of people. Some Astrologers are interested in the history of Astrology, some involve themselves in counselling, or business advice, or Sun sign columns in the media or personality profiling. Some are interested in psychology, health, relationships or politics but all, mostly, are interested in the 'whys' of life and the reasons. They are interested in the *meaning* of life.

Basic Principles

As Nicholas Campion says:

Astrology's character descriptions constitute the world's oldest psychological model and which remains the most widely known form of personality analysis.

When we talk about Sun signs, what we mean is the sign that the

Sun (that big ball of flames) was in on the day the person was born. And Astrology isn't just about the Sun. Along with the Moon and the Sun there are at least nine other celestial bodies in the sky that we observe and plot the paths of as they orbit around the Sun: Mercury, Venus, Mars, Jupiter, Saturn and the three more recent discoveries of Uranus, Neptune and Pluto which I discussed in my books *How to Bond with an Aquarius*, *How to Survive a Pisces* and *How to Win the Trust of a Scorpio* respectively.

Astrology and Astronomy were once the same science but they've now parted company. We still use astronomical data to calculate a birth chart but the difference between astronomers and us is the *meaning* behind those planetary placements.

I work in private practice as an Astrologer and Homeopath. I write from personal experience and am guided by the clients that I see in my practice. People don't come and have a reading or a consultation when they're feeling fit and well. No, they come and see me when they want to get on to their 'Soul Path' or after the break-up of a marriage, or when moving or changing jobs, or are in some sort of heartbreaking situation.

I hope I help the people that come and see me, as what prompted me first working in this field was going to various readers or therapists and needing some help myself.

Most of the things I will be telling you are things I've tried myself and recommended to my clients, so I know they work.

After a time, my publisher sold the foreign rights to a Mind, Body and Spirit publisher in Brazil to be translated into Portuguese, so I'd like to say "Hi" to those readers too.

So, here we are at the 4th sign of the Zodiac – Cancer. Let's learn a little about this sign and how to care for one.

Bath 2012

Chapter One

The Sign of Cancer

Cancer is the 4th sign of the Zodiac. To call someone 'a Cancer' they would have to be born generally between the dates of June 21st and July 21st. I say generally because it does depend on what time of day your Cancer was born and where in the world.

If they were born either on the first day or last day of the sign, double-check with a good astrological website or programme to make sure they actually *are* a Cancer. I can't tell you the number of people I've met who thought they were one sign, and that Astrology was rubbish because nothing seemed to fit them, when in fact they were the sign next door. There is no such thing as a cusp, you are either one sign or another, and you can't be both. But as I'm going to explain how to make an accurate birth/natal chart using a free online resource, you don't have to worry. We'll get the correct information.

The nature of Cancer is very different to all the other signs of the Zodiac. I'm not entirely sure why this is, but I have found that even though they are a Water sign, they're not at all the same as the other two Water signs. I suppose you could say that all the signs are different, but there are a lot of similarities between Sagittarius and Gemini: they're mutable signs, they both like change and they also like travel and conversation.

Cancer seems to be in a league all on its own. Maybe it's because of its ruler, which we will discuss in a minute, or maybe it's because it's the first Water sign of the Zodiac, or maybe, and I think this is more the point, Cancer is *the* most emotional sign and, as a general rule, most people are not very good with emotions.

I was talking to an Aquarius lady yesterday and she was telling me about her Cancer brother and what it was about him that drove her mad. She said there were times when she felt so overcome by the depth and strength of his emotions (when they happened) that she felt as if she were drowning in them.

I thought that was quite an interesting comment. Imagine what it must feel like to be that Cancer person and get those overwhelming feelings and to feel so overcome that other people feel they are drowning in them and nothing else will happen until they subside.

The Moon: Our Nearest Celestial Neighbour

Each sign of the Zodiac has a planet that 'looks after' it. We call it their 'ruler'. The ruler to Cancer is the Moon, that wonderful white disc in the sky at night.

Rather like Cancer the sign, the Moon is deemed in our Western 'modern' world to not be of any great importance. And now that 'man' has landed on the Moon, it seems as if all the wonder associated with this planet has drained away. But many cultures, luckily, still have an affinity with our little satellite.

I have a very basic telescope that I use every now and then, and the first time I used it I managed to see the surface of the Moon. It's a wonderful sight!

Never mind all the other planets out there; the Moon is our nearest neighbour. (The Moon is called a planet in Astrology but technically in astronomy it's called a satellite.) It's had poetry written about it, paintings, songs, religions, and exploration. It's fascinated people since the beginning of time. It certainly fascinates Astrologers because we use the Moon to help us understand a person's emotional make-up. More of that in Chapter Four.

Earliest civilisations have tracked the phases of the Moon, as it's the easiest planet to see with the naked eye. In some cultures the Moon has been worshipped. Rightly so, as without the Moon there would be no reminder for us that we're part of a bigger system, part of a much larger community and one, sadly, we barely understand. Now we're all so focused on our computer screens and TVs and mobile phones, we don't spend much time looking up at the night sky. As dusk approaches we get home by the light of streetlamps, or halogen security lights; but in earlier times, we would have to have either gone to bed at dusk, or used the light of the Moon to guide us if the night sky was clear.

Reflecting the Light

The Moon doesn't produce any light of its own and appears to shine from the reflected light of the Sun. We don't even see all of its surface as *"more than 40 per cent of the lunar surface remains permanently out of view from Earth,"*[3] so we mostly see features on only one side of the Moon. That lunar landscape has barely changed in millions of years because the Moon, unlike the other planets in our Solar System, is devoid of any weather or activity. It is a solid inactive world.

The surface is covered with a soil or dust made up from billions of years of impacts, hence the craters we can see with telescopes, or even on a clear night, with the naked eye. The Moon's gravity is a sixth as strong as the Earth, which is why the Apollo Mission astronauts could bounce around when they left the lunar module. This gravitational pull also causes the tides that raise and lower our seas every day. When the Moon is nearest to the Earth, that side of the Earth closest to the Moon has a high tide, and so does its opposite side.

When the Moon is furthest away, the tides are lower. If you watch time-lapse photography on YouTube (just search 'time-lapse tides') you can be witness to how much the coastline changes in 24 hours. While you're there on the beach, unless you're there all day, you'll miss how far in and out the sea ranges. I expect this is why numerous people have become stranded on beaches when the tide comes in.

Remember this about the Moon, how its effect on the tides can be imperceptible but can overcome you if you're not prepared.

In Astrology we view Water as representing the emotions so equally the Moon-ruled sign of Cancer can seem gentle and sensitive but get them on a 'bad day' and you'll be (and so will they) overcome and/or flooded by their emotions. In other words, you'll both be more sensitized to emotional tidal waves.

Walking on the Moon

Interestingly, one of the last men to walk on the Moon was a man called Harrison Schmitt. Not only was he a Cancer but he was also one of the astronauts who landed on the Moon.

He was so influenced by his experience that he wrote a book called *Return to the Moon: Exploration, Enterprise, and Energy in the Human Settlement of Space*[4] that discusses the pros and cons of actually living on the Moon and what spacesuits and physical examinations and considerations would be necessary for that to happen. No further exploration has been undertaken on the Moon's surface since 1972. Maybe it's time to leave our celestial neighbour alone.

The Moon and Cancers

Some Cancers have 'got in touch' with the Moon, which I think is a very good idea as it helps them feel more 'in the flow'.

Here's Stephanie, a mother to one son, a Pisces. She was born in Germany and came to the UK to work. She's a nurse and part-time therapist. I asked Stephanie her views on the Moon:

I started using a moon calendar quite a while ago. I have to say it works really well for me. I do know now when I have got my strong/energetic periods and the weak ones. For example: I have to write quite a few reports at work and some days I can write every-thing very easily and others, say a week later, I find it difficult. I look on my calendar then and yes, I know why... the moon phase... It's usually when the moon is going to be full soon or a new moon arrives that I am more energetic. By now I almost know automati-

cally what type of moon we are having; the look on the calendar is only a proof then. It made things more clear for me why things sometimes don't run as smooth on one day/week than another. I even cut my nails according to the moon calendar and get sometimes the feeling when it's the right time to do so.

What Makes a Cancer Happy?

Tom is a Cancer and a retired teacher of woodworking and drafting and lives in Minnesota, USA.

I asked him what makes him happy:

Fishing, dancing, playing softball, singing in the choir, our house, cooking, my wife.

Douglas is a Cancer with a Taurus Ascendant and Moon in Aries. He lives and works in Bristol, UK. He is self-employed and lays gas and water mains but the recession has taken its toll as very few new homes are being built and he has to work away from home at lot, something he doesn't enjoy. I asked him what makes him happy and he said he is passionate about skittles and has played it since he was a young man, and his most memorable event was when he won the Singles contest. Skittles is a UK-based game that is mostly played in pubs and involves throwing wooden balls on to the wooden skittles to knock them down. This is a very old pastime and something a Cancer would love *because* it's old-fashioned.

I asked Stephanie what made her happy:

When everything is in peace and harmony, a bunch of flowers, a good cuddle (from my son or husband), spending time with my family, good weather (sunshine, warm temperatures and blue sky), good relationship to my friends and family, good food and cooking.

I loved the way she didn't just say "cuddle" from her husband or son, but a "good" cuddle, as if there are different versions of cuddles! I wonder if Cancers have a cuddle-o-meter that works out inwardly what a good or bad cuddle is? Just after I pondered that question, I found my answer.

In 2007 the Guardian newspaper asked 14 public figures to keep a diary for one week. One of those asked was Cancer actor Diana Rigg (who starred in *The Avengers*).

On day Three (Sunday) she wrote:

Had a date to see Rachael, my daughter, but she's been called away on location, so I'll have to do without a cuddle. We both give good cuddles. I am a great believer in cuddles. Rating people on their cuddlability is fun. I reckon Gordon Brown is a good cuddler, but his mind wouldn't be on it, and one can always tell. David Cameron – too brisk and efficient for comfort. Sir Menzies? Forget it. Zoë Wanamaker, I know, gives good cuddle. I sometimes think of all those OAPs stuck away in homes. How they must long for warm human contact. Dogs, since their beneficial effects have been recognised, are taken to visit; why not a kindly person to dispense cuddles?[5]

The more I read and learned about Cancers, the more I thought I should have titled this book 'How to Cuddle a Cancer'. However, that would probably have been a rather more silly title and also not entirely helpful because it's not just cuddling them that's needed. It's understanding their feelings.

Harriet is a professional development consultant at her local council's customer contact centre. She lives and works in the suburbs of London.

I asked her what makes her happy:

Nothing makes me happier than spending time with people I love. My family and friends mean the world to me. I am a very sociable person and while I consider myself to have lots of 'friends' I have a small number of true friends who I know will always be in my life.

I love spending time at home. I'm a real home bod. I love sleeping, good food and drink, and good film and music. I also love to sing!

As you can tell from this example, Harriet is perfectly happy being at home and with the ones she loves. How un-complex and refreshing that sounds!

Astrologer's Views

To get an idea of what Astrologers say about Cancer, let's ask a few of them their views.

Here's Colin Evans in his *The New Waite's Compendium of Natal Astrology*, published in 1971 but actually written in 1917:

Cancer individuals are very emotional and sensitive, intensely romantic, with vivid imagination. Like the crab, their symbol of the zodiac, they are extremely tenacious... They seem to be drawn to meetings and similar functions where sensation is the main feature... his tense features and excited gestures reflect every ebb and flow of the fortunes of that party, then completely under the sway of sensation he shouts the names of his particular idols, admiringly, coaxingly, fiercely, according to his mood but always in a personal way, though he has never met him in his life... This liability to absorb the nature of others should warn the Cancerian to choose carefully his environment and friends. Deep down within them there is a love of all things mystical and occult, antique and curious. They appreciate home comforts, ease and luxury. Sensitiveness about their families, relations and friends is a very marked feature with them. Retentiveness and tenacity are part of them, and even in the faculty of memory this will be noticed, for they can recall in exact detail minute incidents that have happened many years ago.[6]

Hmm. Sounds quite revealing. Are all Cancers like this?

Let's ask Adrian Duncan (who is an Astrologer and a Cancer), author of the *World of Wisdom* Astrological program:

> *The bond to your mother will have been particularly formative. You are sensitive and easily hurt – though this may not be immediately apparent on the outside. Likewise, you are loyal and passionate in your defence of those you love – injury done to them is also done to you. You have a strong and instinctive protective nature... You have a great talent for building up a nurturing environment for those who are close to you, yet it can also help to be more open to those who are not necessarily so close. You are easily upset by changes in your daily rhythm, and can be rather grumpy when called upon to change habitual behaviours. Your home is your castle.[7]*

I'd agree with these sentiments.

Let's ask a female astrologer now. Will she have a different view?

Here's Rae Orion in her *Astrology for Dummies*:

> *Ruled by the ever-changing Moon, you are responsive, aware, a creature of many moods. But though you sometimes feel adrift on an ocean of emotion, you are determined to achieve your goals – and you generally do.[8]*

And here's Linda Goodman in her *Linda Goodman's Sun Signs* in 1968:

> *His tears are never crocodile tears. They flow from the deep rivers of his fragile and vulnerable heart. You can wound his sensitive feelings with a harsh glance or a rough tone of voice. Cruelty can bring on brimming eyes or a complete withdrawal... in the midst of uncertainty, despair and sadness, Cancer people seek retreat and solitude. Just like real crabs.[9]*

Lastly let's check with Felix Lyle and Bryan Aspland in their

Instant Astrologer:

> Cancer: protective, tenacious, imaginative, sensitive, nostalgic, tough, clannish, touchy, clinging, possessive, shrewd, caring, manipulative, intuitive, devious, fearful, dependent.[10]

I think it's safe to say that the Sun sign Cancer's main keywords are mothering/nurturing, moody and emotional, homely and family orientated.

Mothering/Nurturing

The Cancers I know (and there are quite a few, I also have a nephew and a niece) definitely like to nurture and 'look after' people and animals. They're the ones that people go to, to tell them their problems, get a hug if they're down, will look after your pet or your baby with open arms, and will enjoy being needed.

ALL Cancers that I've ever met have a strong link with their mothers or main carer. Even if they don't get on with them that well, they still crave the gentle touch of that person who will nurture them. If a Cancer comes to see me and their mother has died, alarm bells are ringing…

Here the UK pop star George Michael tells us what happened after his mother died:

> *I struggled with huge depression after my mother died. Losing your mother and your lover in the space of three years is a tough one.*

Harriet tells us about her relationship with her mother:

> *As well as her being a wonderfully kind, loving and ever supportive person, we also get on as friends. We have very similar personalities and laugh a lot together! Although Mum is definitely more assertive*

than I am. I tell her everything, and nothing beats a cuddle with Mum, I don't know what I'd do without her!

Stephanie's mother is also Pisces (so is her son) and lives in Germany. Here she tells us about their relationship:

I have a good relationship with my mum, who is a Pisces. I do struggle sometimes with her when it comes to making decisions: Mum, I have seen a good flight for you on these particular dates, don't you want to come? Her answer would be: I don't know yet, we could wait and see if we get a better one, it's still time to go… and suddenly she rings and says she's booked a flight, a completely different one and different dates. She always needs time to think about things. She can be very motherly and be a friend at same time. She has been always there for me when I needed her, which I think makes a good trusting relationship.

Both of these ladies have mums that are compatible Astrologically, Harriet's mum is a Virgo, which is an Earth sign (see my *How to Soothe a Virgo* for more info) and Stephanie's mum is a Pisces (see my *How to Survive a Pisces*) and Water and Earth get on nicely, so do fellow Water signs. That's not to say that everyone who's Water or Earth will get on with everyone else who's Water and Earth, but it does help with understanding and empathy.

It increases the odds on getting along well.

A Cancer even if they're not a Mum/Mom themselves will nurture and 'look after' those in their immediate vicinity. The rest of the family, or siblings or little cousins or nephews and this can stretch to their work. I know Cancer ladies who aren't married, but they still manage to 'mother' those they work with, and other members of their family. This is because they enjoy mothering, being mothered, being cared-for, so people tend to treat others how they like to be treated themselves… and Cancers love to care.

Sometimes this can create an inner conflict in your Cancer if their Moon (which we will learn more about in Chapter Four) is in a sign that doesn't quite gel with their Sun sign.

Here's Donna Cunningham, a wonderful astrologer and author, talking about the pluses and minuses of being a Cancer. What do you love about being a Cancer? What do you hate about being a Cancer?

I have a tight square between my reclusive 12th house Cancer Sun and my adventuresome Aries Moon on the Midheaven. My Aries Moon doesn't like my Cancer Sun very much, too whiny and timid, whereas my Cancer Sun is often overwhelmed and intimidated by the rash actions and impetuous demands of my Aries Moon.

I've worked for over 40 years to overcome the negative qualities of Cancer, such as being hypersensitive, hung up in the past, and all that angst about family. It seems like I'm perennially immature, and I really dislike that in myself. Not to mention being too attached to food. Just for today, I'm not in love with anything about being a Cancer. I am NOT motherly.[11]

Maybe Donna isn't motherly in a literal sense, but she's worked all her life helping and caring for people. She has a Masters Degree in social work, was a director of social services in a Brooklyn hospital, and was licensed as a social worker in New York and California. She has over 40 years of private practice experience, counselling clients using astrology, psychology, spirituality and common sense. If that isn't nurturing, I don't know what is!

Moody/Emotional

They say it is better to be poor and happy than rich and miserable, but how about a compromise like moderately rich and just moody?
Princess Diana

This can be a bit of a complaint from other signs about Cancer, that they're moody and emotional. In their defence, I think it's important that they *do* have these traits, as otherwise the world would be a very barren landscape, with no feelings.

This moodiness can manifest as being tearful, to which a lot of Cancers confessed.

Here's Harriet again:

I am very emotional and am well known by family and friends as a weepy and tearful person! I do cry very easily, whether it be because I am happy, sad or otherwise, and during my menstrual cycle this increases 10 fold! I remember one occasion where someone asked me if I wanted a drink, and because I couldn't decide I burst into tears!!

Also, it has only been in the last year that I have gotten better with crying when I get angry – anger always used to manifest as uncontrollable tears which made trying to confront anyone a real challenge (and very frustrating – which then just added to more tears!).

A long time ago now, when I worked in retailing, one of my work colleagues was a Cancer. Every month she became a wobbly blob of wobbliness, and she would have days 'off sick' because of her monthly cycle. I witnessed her getting faint and floppy once and was glad she didn't come into work often like that, as we would have had to keep her in the first aid room all day and keep an eye on her, which is difficult when you're looking after staff, writing rosters, keeping customers happy etc.

When she became a mother though, that whole problem changed and she took to her new role like a duck to water...

Stephanie put it more succinctly:

I am very emotional and cry easily.

This emotional-ness can be a blessing and a curse. Here is Janine.

She manages her own family-run business in Edinburgh selling handmade oriental weaving.

Well you've got to tune into their feelings. Lots of people don't do that. They're not seeing or feeling or experiencing our emotional sides. You have to touch a Cancerian and look into their eyes literally, tune in to what they're feeling and ask them: 'How are you feeling?' Holding them, hugging them.

She told me how sometimes when she was a child, she'd fall out with her mother, who would make her go to her room. A big No-No, as then she felt even more abandoned and misunderstood. Her crying would increase and she wasn't allowed downstairs until she'd pulled herself together. She said it could all have been avoided if her mother had let her talk about how she felt, and in the talking she would have recovered her emotional balance. She said she's the only member of her family who does the hugging (a lot of them are Air signs) and a gentle touch and an arm round her makes her feel supported and 'at home'. Now if anyone she knows feels upset, or weepy she immediately gives them a gentle hug and lets them cry on her shoulder. She does this automatically.

The House, the Home and Family

One never reaches home, but wherever friendly paths intersect the whole world looks like home for a time.
Hermann Hesse

Home definitely is where the heart is for a Cancer. Richard Branson is a UK entrepreneur who started his business life running Virgin records and now also runs or owns shares in railway, airline and entertainment companies totalling more than 400 altogether.

He says:

I cannot remember a moment in my life when I have not felt the love of my family. We were a family that would have killed for each other – and we still are.

Various Cancers I spoke to all had views/thoughts and feelings about their home and family.

Charlotte is an Aquarius surrounded by Cancers. Her late father was a Cancer. She told me how:

He used to say that the best part of a holiday was coming home. I think he did once have to spend a week away and didn't enjoy it one bit.

She also has a Cancer brother who, although he's happy to work away from home, when he is in his house:

He's always making things, and has created an amazing workshop at home; also arty, and has arty and crafty things plus gadgets (mainly ones he's made himself) and computer stuff.

Her now sadly deceased friend Rowland:

Had his favourite 'toys' at home, such as a large model railway set up in his attic and a home organ which he enjoyed playing, and also loved entertaining friends.

It doesn't matter what social strata your Cancer hails from, there is still a strong bond to family. Even Princess Diana the ex-wife of Prince Charles is reported to have said:

Family is the most important thing in the world.

This wanting to recreate their home life at their place of work or with friends can manifest in strange ways.

Tom, who we met earlier, is a retired teacher of woodworking and drafting and lives in Minnesota, USA. His wife told me a little about his compassionate side:

> *He does want to feed the world and sympathizes with those who do not have enough to eat. He tells stories about how he gave lunch money to friends in high school or brought them home for dinner at his house. He volunteers in a food pantry now.*

How practical! How thoughtful! To bring a school friend home for meals if he thought they were needy. I know another Cancer young man who would rather take the blame when his friends fall out with each other than have them arguing. Cancers, as a Water sign, aren't great at arguing. Leave that to the Air and Fire signs, they love a good 'debate'!

Chapter Two

How to Make a Chart

Making a birth chart, or natal chart as they call it in America, is much easier now with the advent of computers. What has complicated the process is the vast amount of information that your computer programme or website will give you.

Everyday I'll have an e-mail from someone who has very cleverly managed to make their own chart online and now they want to know *what it all means.*

For the purposes of this book, you don't need to know too much, just enough to help you feel confident in understanding a little bit about Astrology and the Cancer in your life.

There are three important pieces of information you will need before you start. They are the date, the time and the location of your Cancer's birth.

We need to know the date, because that will tell us if your Cancer actually is a Cancer. If they were born between the dates of June 22nd to July 23rd, they're more likely to be a Cancer. But be careful, if they were born on those starting or ending dates themselves, their location and time of birth might change things.

I'll give you an example:

Mrs Smith was born in Ballen in Denmark on the 22nd June 1921, at 00.17am. That's just into the day... very early in the morning. She's a Gemini, with a Pisces Ascendant and Moon in Capricorn.

Her friend Mrs Brown was born on the same date at exactly the same time in Brisbane in Australia, but she's a Gemini with an Aries Ascendant and Moon in Capricorn.

Their other friend Mr White was born, again on the same date, same time but his place of birth was in a hospital in New York, NY, USA.

Mr White is a Cancer, with a Pisces Ascendant and Moon in Capricorn.

Even though these three births were on the same day, same year, same time but different locations, two of them are Geminis and one is a Cancer, two have the same Ascendant but different Sun signs, and all of them have their Moon in Capricorn.

To make this easier to understand, you have to imagine for a moment that the little map of the heavens we're going to make of your Cancer's birth is as if we were looking up at the sky on the day of birth... and us here on the Earth are part of a much bigger place = the Universe. And in our little spot of the Universe, we are all orbiting around the Sun. So looking at the sky from Brisbane in Australia is different from looking at it in Ballen in Denmark.

Astrologers use astronomical information and you can bless your lucky stars that you don't have to calculate all the degrees of longitude and latitude and make your brain go to fuzz doing that... just let the website's software do all that calculation.

If you were born in Scotland, your Cancer's birth time will be on their birth certificate. Unfortunately, if you were born in the UK, no such helpful information will automatically be there, unless you're a twin. If you're lucky the hospital record might still exist, or mother or father might remember, and if you're extremely lucky (which I am) you'll have a relative who's into Astrology and they've recorded the time.

If you were born in the USA again, you're lucky as your birth time will be on your birth certificate.

As there are so many websites to choose from, we're going to use one that I use myself, so we know it's accurate and free.

Go to www.astro.com and make an account.

They will ask for your e-mail and nothing else (unless you want to add it).

You can create a chart as a 'guest user' or do what I recommend which is create a 'free registered user profile'. This means every time you log in, the site will know it's you and it makes life much easier. Plus astro.com (called Astrodienst which means 'Astro Service') is a website real, live Astrologers use. It has over 6 million visitors per month and over 16,000 forum members, so you will be in good company.

Input all your data.

You will need to know the time, the place and the location of the Cancer in your life.

If you're not sure of the time, just use 6am, but you'll have to skip Chapters Three and Five about the houses and the Ascendant.

After you have entered all your data –

Date
Time
Location of birth

– we can now get your chart made.

Go to the page marked 'free horoscopes' and scroll down the page until you see the section marked:

Extended Chart Selection

Click on this link and you'll be taken to a page that's got lots of boxes but the main headings on the left are:

Birth Data
Methods
Options
Image size
Additional objects

Add all your info into the boxes if you haven't already, then click on the section marked House System under the heading Options.

Scroll down until you see 'equal' and click on that. This makes your chart into equal segments, and is the system this book is based on. If you don't do that because you're in a hurry or can't be bothered, then the information in Chapter Five will be wrong. The default system on this website, and most websites and computer programmes (except the ones I use!) are set to a system called Placidus. This makes each house (which we will learn about in Chapter Five) unequal sizes... and to my mind looks scraggy and uneven.

Plus the Equal House system is the oldest system and the one the ancients used before Mr Placidus came along and made some changes.

Now click the blue button 'Click here to show the chart' and 'bing'!! Your chart will appear in another window.

At first look, it will all seem like gobbledygook; but don't worry, we don't need too much information.

In the centre of your chart, you will see the numbers 1–12. These are called the houses and are arranged in an anticlockwise order.

These are the shapes representing the signs, so find the one that matches yours. They are called glyphs.

Aries ♈
Taurus ♉
Gemini ♊
Cancer ♋
Leo ♌
Virgo ♍
Libra ♎
Scorpio ♏
Sagittarius ♐
Capricorn ♑
Aquarius ♒
Pisces ♓

The Elements

To understand your Cancer fully, you must take into account which Element their Ascendant and Moon are in.

Each sign of the Zodiac has been given an element that it operates under: Earth, Air, Fire and Water. I like to think of them as operating at different 'speeds'.

The **Earth** signs are **Taurus, Virgo** and **Capricorn**. The Earth Element is stable, grounded and concerned with practical matters. A Cancer with a lot of Earth in their chart works best at a very slow, steady speed. (I refer to these in the text as 'Earthy'.)

The **Air** signs are **Gemini, Libra** and **Aquarius** (who is the 'Water-carrier' *not* a Water sign). The Air element enjoys ideas, concepts and thoughts. It operates at a faster speed than Earth, not as fast as Fire but faster than Water and Earth. Imagine them as being medium speed. (I refer to these as Airy or Air signs.)

The **Fire** signs are **Aries, Leo** and **Sagittarius**. The Fire element likes action, excitement and can be very impatient. Their speed is *very* fast. (I refer to these as Firey i.e. Fire-Sign.)

The **Water** signs are our friend **Cancer**, and the other two: **Scorpio** and **Pisces**. The Water element involves feelings, impressions, hunches and intuition. They operate faster than Earth but not as fast as Air. A sort of slow-medium speed. (I refer to these as Watery or Water signs.)

Chapter Three

The Ascendant

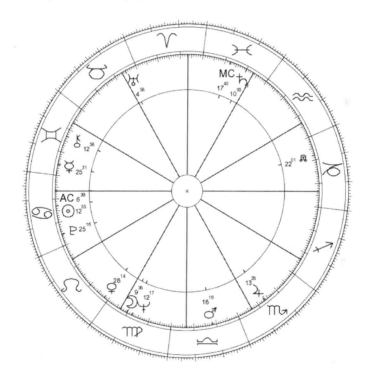

Name: ♂ Dalai Lama
born on Sa., 6 July 1935
in Tengster/Qinhai, CHINA
101e12, 36n32

Time: 4:38 a.m.
Univ.Time: 21:38 5 July
Sid. Time: 23:14.36

ASTRO DIENST
www.astro.com

Type: 2.GR 0.0-1 17-Sep-2012

Natal Chart (Method: Liz Greene / equal)

As you now know how to make a chart, you now need to learn a
little about the major parts of the chart. Let's look at the Sample
Chart above of the Dalai Lama.

The Ascendant is determined by the time of birth, and
changes every 2 hours or so. If your Cancer was born at 6am,
they will have a different Ascending or Rising sign to someone
born at 2pm.

This is because the Earth moves around the Sun in its orbit and our 'view' of the horizon changes. We don't change, but the bit of the sky that we can see on the eastern horizon changes every few minutes and changes signs every 2 hours, as there are 12 signs of the Zodiac, and 360 degrees in a circle... and obviously, as the Earth is a sort of globe hanging in space, and we're orbiting around the Sun at any given moment, the bit of the galaxy we are travelling through also changes.

Nothing in nature is static. What *is* static is your birth chart because it represents the location of the planets in the sky on the day and time you were born and as such is a wonderful record of that planetary moment. A bit like a Cosmic Fingerprint. It's never going to change. What does change is where the planets are now... but that's another bit of astrology called transits, which I haven't got space to go into here.

The Ascendant is your moment of birth, the actual time that you came out of the womb.

If you imagine a person standing on a beach, looking out to sea, what they are looking at on the horizon would be the Ascendant. So it's really Astrological shorthand for the horizon.

This can seem a little strange to an Astrological newbie. There you are thinking knowing your Star sign, or Astrological or even Zodiac sign was enough. That this was all there was to know. It isn't. Now you are opening the door to the wonderful world of Astrology and all we're learning here is some basics, but they will stand you in good stead it you want to explore the subject further and walk in the steps of people like Carl Jung, or John Dee astrologer to Queen Elizabeth the 1st, or William Lilly... the list is very long.

The Ascendant in the birth chart is where your chart starts and as it's determined by your actual time of birth, it's quite auspicious. We know the Sun spends roughly a month in each sign; well, the Ascendant changes signs every 2 hours or so which is why having the correct birth time is important.

Astrologers view the Ascendant sign as being how you 'see' the world, the glasses you wear (are they rose-tinted in Taurus or dark red in Scorpio?). As it's your actual time of birth, it's how you tackle things in a crisis, your knee-jerk reaction to things, how you came into the world.

Someone with a Capricorn Ascendant is totally different to someone with a Leo Ascendant, even if they're both Cancerians.

In our example chart, you will see the initials AC at the ¼ 9 position in the chart. AC is short for Ascendant. The line dissects the sign that looks like two 6s, which is the sign of Cancer, so the Dalai Lama's Ascendant is Cancer. His view of the world is the same as his Sun sign's view, which is about nurturing and caring. Which I think perfectly describes the Dalai Lama, as not only is he a peace warrior, but his spiritual writings are all about caring for others, not just ourselves. He also was incredibly upset when he had to leave his place of birth in Tibet and go to Dharamsala in northern India to escape persecution. He still is working to bring peace to Tibet, his home.

Girls, if you're dating, that first eyes-meet-across-the-room feeling will be coming from yours (and his) Ascendant. This is why two people with the same Sun sign might seem completely different when you first meet them… this is because all you experience is their Ascendant, or Rising sign.

Here are the various Ascendants that your Cancer could have. I've included some quotes from people who we know were born with that Ascendant sign and are all Cancers, and you'll grasp as you read that each one expresses their Ascendant sign quite nicely.

Aries Ascendant

Decide that you want it more than you are afraid of it.
Bill Cosby

As the first sign of the Zodiac and one represented by the Ram, Aries Ascendant will incline one to be the leader, mover and shaker in their life. They enjoy rapid decisions, swift action, and decisiveness and are fearless in their desires. They view life as a challenge to be fought and won.

Taurus Ascendant

Tell the truth, work hard, and come to dinner on time.
Gerald R. Ford

The Earth element of Taurus gives your Cancer a slower approach, more centred on the body and physical things such as food and sustenance. They see their life through glasses aimed at that which can be eaten or experienced physically. By the body, for the body and through the body.

Gemini Ascendant

A computer would deserve to be called intelligent if it could deceive a human into believing that it was human.
Alan Turing

Inquisitive Gemini, the eternal child, asks the questions of life that others might not even think about. They use the eternal 'why' and will see their life as a place to explore and find answers. They love all forms of communication and love to keep in touch with everyone and everything.

Cancer Ascendant

We can live without religion and meditation, but we cannot survive without human affection.
Dalai Lama

As the same sign as their Sun, the Cancer Ascendant will approach their life wanting to be part of one big family where everyone gets on and welcomes feelings and emotions. If they are cared for correctly they can rise to amazing spiritual and monetary heights. They love all forms of life, the fluffier the better.

Leo Ascendant

I do expose my body, but only because I think people should have something nice to look at.
Brigitte Nielsen

As a Fire sign and one that loves an adoring audience, there is less shyness and more ability to shine and show off. They want to be included and respected and see their life's mission to be demonstrative and dramatic. They are warm, friendly and affectionate provided they're not ignored.

Virgo Ascendant

There is no rule on how to write. Sometimes it comes easily and perfectly; sometimes it's like drilling rock and then blasting it out with charges.
Ernest Hemingway

As an Earth sign and ruled by Mercury, this Ascendant is concerned with detail, analysis and perfection. Good at communicating and wanting to find the perfect way to do things. They enjoy good health and prefer things to be ordered and organised.

Libra Ascendant

My life really began when I married my husband.
Nancy Reagan

Ruled by Venus the goddess of love here we have a desire to be united in a partnership or close relationship. Renowned for indecision and the desire for emotional balance as represented by the scales, that can swing up or down. Balance is the best solution.

Scorpio Ascendant

Stand-ups are fearless in that way. In the early days when Mork and Mindy *was on TV, it was an anti-Mork, where I could do something slightly darker and crazier.*
Robin Williams

This deep, dark emotional sign as an Ascendant needs to trust to feel contented. Ruled by Pluto the planet of power and transformation, there is no getting past their X-ray ability to see deep into your soul. Famed for the strength of their deep focus.

Sagittarius Ascendant

I have always believed, and I still believe, that whatever good or bad fortune may come our way we can always give it meaning and transform it into something of value.
Hermann Hesse

Another Fire sign, Sagittarius is ruled by benevolent Jupiter the upbeat God of gods. Eternally optimistic and aiming for a place where their arrows have shot to the heights, they are searching for a deeper meaning to their life.

Capricorn Ascendant

It is not the mountain we conquer but ourselves.
Edmund Hillary

As Saturn is their stern ruler, a Cancer with Capricorn Ascendant is pragmatic, down to earth and ambitious. The family is the centre of their world. They want practical solutions to problems, money in the bank and a firm grasp on life's difficulties. On a good day their sense of humour is vast; on a bad day grey clouds block their view and can make them seem grumpy old beings.

Aquarius Ascendant

We have to free half of the human race, the women, so that they can help to free the other half.
Emmeline Pankhurst

Ruled by crazy Uranus, the planet that wants to 'be different', Aquarius Ascendant is an Air sign wants to breeze through life's problems by searching for the alternative answers. Cerebral and thought based they can seem less emotionally connected than their Sun sign Cancer. If it's different they will do it and freedom is a must!

Pisces Ascendant

Watching a peaceful death of a human being reminds us of a falling star; one of a million lights in a vast sky that flares up for a brief moment only to disappear into the endless night forever.
Elisabeth Kübler-Ross

As one of the more sensitive signs and ruled by psychic Neptune, Pisces wants to play with the fairies and angels and leave the painful, hurtful world behind. More likely to be disorganised, but are truly empathic. They gaze at life through kindly, blurry spectacles.

Chapter Four

The Moon

*The Moon denotes the instincts, the subconscious, the desire-nature
and the feelings and reactions.*
Colin Evans

In Astrology the Moon represents how we feel about things. If the
Sun represents our ego and our conscious self, then the Moon,
just as in real life, reflects the light of the Sun and in Astrology
represents how we reflect or feel about things.

In 1953 a French psychologist called Michel Gauquelin
(Scorpio Sun, Leo Ascendant and Moon in Sagittarius) did some
statistical work. He spent a number of years analysing the birth
data of over 20,000 doctors, famous actors, writers, politicians
and sports people and found an uncanny significance with the
placement of various planets on the days they were born. Now
whether or not you believe the statistics he researched and
published, there is no doubt he came across some interesting
phenomena and I (personally) think his work should be
celebrated.

He studied Saturn, Jupiter and Venus and also the Moon and
it's this bit of his work we're going to explore.

Michel was of the opinion that if the Moon was rising (near
the Ascendant) or directly overhead on the day someone was
born, or below or at right angles, they were more likely to be
artistic, creative, loving of poetry, dreamy, sensitive, rather sweet
and impressionable. He also found a lot of writers and authors
had this signature.

Now, this isn't to say that everyone who has their Moon
placed on their Ascendant or in their 4th, 7th, 9th or 10th houses
will actually *become* a writer or author but the odds are in favour

of this happening. I didn't know this when I started to write my book series, but I do have my Moon in the 10th house... so there might be some truth in this.

The Moon takes about 28 days to circuit the Earth (27 days, 7 hours, 43 minutes, 11.6 seconds to be exact)... as we circuit round the Sun. During those 28 days it spends around 2 days in each sign of the Zodiac. As the Moon doesn't know about days and weeks and hours, its sign-changing doesn't quite correspond to our days of the week.

If you look at an Ephemeris, the astronomical calculations of the planets' placements throughout each month in the signs, you'll see how the Moon changes signs. The astro.com website has a page of over 2,000 years of data, so you can track the Moon and other planets backwards and forwards from your date of birth, which if you're interested in Astrology, can be fascinating.

I'll give you a little example. As I'm writing this passage, the Sun is just going into the sign of Libra at exactly 15.48 today. In just over a week's time, the Moon will be full and will be in the Sun's *opposite* sign of Aries. Last month, when the Sun was in Virgo, the Moon was 'full' in the sign of Pisces. The full Moon is when the Moon is totally visible, with no bits missing due to the Earth's shadow.

The next time you see a full Moon, you will know it is *'in the sign of'* the opposite Sun sign.

These are things you will need to know to be happy with the Cancer in your life. You need to know the ebbing and flowing of the Moon's visibility to us here on Earth.

In the following examples, the people with Moon in Capricorn will have been born when the Moon was full, and as they're a Cancer all those moon-like feelings will be intensified for them every full Moon.

Now, all of this is fine and dandy on a good day when you've got your wits about you. What happens if your Moon is in a sign that isn't quite compatible to your Sun sign? You'll be thinking one thing, and feeling something else, and it really helps to get a grasp of the two issues, so you can feel calm and at peace.

If your Cancer has, say, Moon in Sagittarius, which is a Fire sign, they might want to travel and go back to university and talk late into the night about Life, the Universe and Everything, and on other days will just want to stay at home and snuggle-up on the sofa... and there you are wondering, "How they can be so fickle?" They're not. It's just that their Astrological make-up comprises of something more than their Sun sign and all the bits of the chart need to be acknowledged, understood and embraced.

To find what sign your Cancer's Moon is in, go back and look at their chart and find the Moon symbol ☽ and find out what sign it is in, then have a read of the relevant descriptions below.

The Dr Bach Flower Essences

In 1933 Dr Edward Bach, a medical doctor and Homeopath, published a little booklet called *The Twelve Healers and Other Remedies*. His theory was that if the emotional component a person was suffering from was removed, their 'illness' would also disappear. I tend to agree with this kind of thinking as most illnesses (except being hit by a bus) are preceded by an unhappy event or an emotional disruption that then sets into place the body getting out of sync. Removing the emotional issue and bringing a bit of stability into someone's life, when they are having a hard time, can improve their overall health so much that wellness resumes.

Knowing which Bach Flower Essence can help certain worries and upsetments gives you and your Cancer more control over your lives. I recommend the essences a lot in my practice if I feel a certain part of a person's chart is under stress... and usually it's the Moon that needs help. The essences describe the negative aspects of the character, which are focused on during treatment. This awareness helps reverse those trends, so when our emotional selves are nice and comfortable, we can then face each day with more strength.

I've quoted Dr Bach's actual words for each sign.

To use the essences take 2 drops from the stock bottle and put it into a glass of water and sip. I tend to recommend putting them into a small water bottle, and sipping them throughout the day, at least 4 times. For young children, do the same.

Remember to seek medical attention if symptoms don't get better and/or seek professional counselling.

Aries Moon

My childhood was fun, safe, wild and mischievous.
Aimée Ann Duffy

As a Fire sign, and first sign of the Zodiac, Aries is all about 'me'. They will need to feel that the world revolves around their feelings, so not so good at sharing or compromise. It has the added benefit though of being completely truthful, so if you ask an Aries Moon how they are feeling and they tell you, they're being totally honest.

Bach Flower Essence Impatiens:

Those who are quick in thought and action and who wish all things to be done without hesitation or delay.

Taurus Moon

Instant gratification is not soon enough.
Meryl Streep

Grounded in the reality of the Earth and all its pleasures, Taurus Moon will want nice tasty food, stable finances, and raunchy sex. Taste is important, as are the kinaesthetic senses of touch, so soft fluffy clothing, velvet/silk/satin and things that feel pleasant are incredibly important. They won't say "No" to good wine and chocolate either, and as a slower sign will develop gradually. Don't rush them!

Bach Flower Essence Gentian:

Those who are easily discouraged. They may be progressing well in the affairs of their daily life, but any small delay or hindrance to progress causes doubt and soon disheartens them.

Gemini Moon

One advantage in keeping a diary is that you become aware with reassuring clarity of the changes which you constantly suffer.
Franz Kafka

Oh, the eternal child! Gemini never wants to grow old! This is the Moon sign of two options and opinions, as they are the astrological twins. They like discussion, argument, conversation and for things to be (as this is an Air sign) cerebral and swift. Short journeys are loved too.

Bach Flower Essence Cerato:

Those who have not sufficient confidence in themselves to make their own decisions.

Cancer Moon

It's my mother's engagement ring so I thought it was quite nice because obviously she's not going to be around to share any of the fun and excitement of it all – this was my way of keeping her close to it all.
Prince William

The Cancer Moon is happiest when they can feel their emotions and feel safe, nurtured, cuddled and snuggled. As Cancer is 'ruled' by the Moon it's in its home sign. They can be cranky and moody but equally they will love deeply. They will also love Mum/Mom, the home and home delights and all things aged and traditional.

Bach Flower Essence Clematis:

Living in the hopes of happier times, when their ideals may come true.

Leo Moon

I love what I do. I take great pride in what I do. And I can't do something halfway, three-quarters, nine-tenths. If I'm going to do something, I go all the way.

Tom Cruise

When the Moon goes into Leo, things hot up. It's a cheery, optimistic Moon but ignore it at your peril! They love to bask in the glow of the love from their entourage, enjoy the red-carpet treatment, wince if you forget their name and love you if you thank them profusely for their kindness, which will be great.

Bach Flower Essence Vervain:

Those with fixed principles and ideas, which they are confident are right.

Virgo Moon

I can't worry about moral outrage.

Willem Dafoe

Here we have the sign that could get a qualification in worrying.

They worry about this, they worry about that, they then worry about worrying and so it goes on. On a good day their powers of analysis and classification are a joy and they have an enormous memory for irrelevant information. They will happily dot every 'I' and cross every 'T' and remind you that you said this and that on certain dates. Encyclopaedias and libraries are well starred too.

Bach Flower Essence Centaury:

Their good nature leads them to do more than their own share of work and they may neglect their own mission in life.

Libra Moon

I've always been a serial monogamist.
Kristen Bell

This is the classic sign of indecision represented by the scales that form the sign of Libra. Should I do this? Or that? Or the other thing? Their concerns will centre around close personal relationships and they are at their happiest with a ring on their finger and someone to love. Fairness and balance are also important.

Bach Flower Essence Scleranthus:

Those who suffer from being unable to decide between two things, first one seeming right then the other.

Scorpio Moon

I learned that courage was not the absence of fear, but the triumph over it. The brave man is not he who does not feel afraid, but he who conquers that fear.
Nelson Mandela

If you think of the colour deep, deep red you'll get an idea of what it's like to have a Scorpio Moon. Deep feelings, deep thoughts and even deep resentments if they're frustrated in their desires. There are no half-measures. All, or nothing. They will stick through thick and thin if they're on your side. They will stop at nothing if you're not. Not a combination to trifle with.

Bach Flower Essence Chicory:

They are continually correcting what they consider wrong and enjoy doing so.

Sagittarius Moon

I spent a lot of time in New York in the 1980s with the downtown arts crowd.
Marc Almond

As a Fire sign and one of the more swift-speed Moons, Sagittarius Moon wants to answer all of life's questions, or at least ask them and investigate them. Any sort of learning or teaching will keep them amused as will contact with foreign countries and other civilisations. On the downside, they love to 'be right' so be careful not challenge their beliefs too much.
This essence comes under the heading 'Over-Sensitive to Influences and Ideas'.

Bach Flower Essence Agrimony:

They hide their cares behind their humour and jesting and try to bear their trials with cheerfulness.

Capricorn Moon

The world breaks everyone, and afterward, some are strong at the broken places.
Ernest Hemingway

Strict Saturn, the planet of 'hard-knocks', rules Capricorn. They will learn at an early age that life isn't always fluffy and fun. They will prefer serious subjects, sensible ideas and life built on firm foundations. They will also put up with more than any other sign and be stoic in how they tackle life's challenges.

Bach Flower Essence Mimulus:

Fear of worldly things, illness, pain, accident, poverty, of dark, of being alone, of misfortune. They secretly bear their dread and do not speak freely of it to others.

Aquarius Moon

I am a free spirit, unfortunately for some.
Princess Diana

Friendship with a capital 'F' rules Aquarius. For a Cancer it reduces slightly their emotional deepness and allows weird and wonderful ideas and friendships to be born. Full of ideas and crazy thoughts they will draw you into their world view, which is inclusive and utopian. Whether or not they are happy as a human being is debatable. Spock from *Star Trek* comes to mind, but fun they certainly can be.

Bach Flower Essence Water Violet:

For those who like to be alone, very independent, capable and self-reliant. They are aloof and go their own way.

Pisces Moon

The best and most beautiful things in the world cannot be seen or even touched – they must be felt with the heart.
Helen Keller

As the last sign of the Zodiac and one that is supremely sensitive to fairies, angels, and all things spiritual and other-worldly, a Cancer with Moon in Pisces will have a slightly longer road to travel to get to contentment. As the sign of the martyr, they can, on a bad day, imagine all the suffering in the world, which will make them feel weak and low. On a good day they will sense you are trying to reach them, imagine (correctly) how you are feeling and will 'be there' for you in this life and the next. Just make sure you guide them back to earth occasionally…

Bach Flower Essence Rock Rose:

For cases where there even appears no hope or when the person is very frightened or terrified.

Chapter Five

The Houses

It's more difficult to explain what house is if you haven't actually ever made a birth chart. It's only when you make more than one chart that you realise all the different bits end up in different places. Those different places are what we call the houses. They used to be called Mansions as they are home for each planet.

In our example chart the Dalai Lama has his Sun located in the first house. This is because he was born just as the Sun was rising, so in our little map of the heavens his Sun is near where the chart starts. And as we discussed in Chapter Three the chart starts at the Ascendant point.

When we make a chart we do it in an anticlockwise manner (counter clockwise) so the houses go from one to 12 all the way round the circle. What time of day your Cancer was born determines which house their Sun will fall into.

You can check a chart is correct by imagining that the horizontal line going from left to right dissecting the chart is the horizon. So if your Cancer was born during the day their Sun *should* be located above the horizon in the upper part of the chart.

Don't worry about this too much if it doesn't make any sense, as all you really need to know is that their Sun could be in any one of the 12 houses. Provided you've made your chart using the correct time the Sun will 'be' in the correct house. And as there are 12 houses it could be in any one of them.

Look for the symbol ☉ in the chart that you have made and see which numbered section it has ended up in, then read the description below. You will, obviously, only need to read the description that relates to the chart you have made; but when you start making other people's charts, you'll notice their Sun might be in another house.

So what is the *meaning* of having the Sun in different placements? Well, we think of each house being a bit like each sign of the Zodiac. So the first house is a little like the sign of Aries, and so on. Having the Sun in the first house is totally different to having it in the 7th house, as the first is all about 'me' and the 7th is all about 'others'.

The placement of the Sun modifies its expression. It doesn't change 'who' that person is; they're still motivated by all those Cancer qualities we've discussed already but they express them differently.

This is where having your birth chart made up makes astrology totally individual to you. As there are 12 houses, and we're just using the Sun's location (In a full chart you'd be taking into account at least 8 other planets and the Moon AND making sense of it all!!) we're keeping it as easy as possible.

In my chart I've got my Sun in the sign of Pisces in the 7th house, but my mother (who I wrote about in *How to Bond with an Aquarius*) has her Sun in the sign of Aquarius, in the 9th.

We've both got Moon in Gemini, so we love to yak, but where we're 'going' in life is different.

Where your Sun is located is where you feel 'at home'. Where you like to spend your life focus the most. If your Sun is in the 3rd, you'll like writing or chatting or teaching or anything associated with the 3rd house but if your husband or significant other has their Sun in the 8th, they're going to want to keep a bit of themselves secret and will like to get deeply involved in things.

There are more than one House System. I use Equal House but most people use Placidus, so unless you make your chart using the Equal House system my interpretations won't be the same. I must point out that there is no agreement among Astrologers to what is the 'correct' system. You have to find the one you like the most.

The First House, House of Personality

No matter what behaviour you are seeking to change, you need to start by developing a strong willingness or wish to do it.
Dalai Lama

Having the Cancer Sun in the first house ensures personal confidence as it relates to the 'self', in sort of an 'I am the centre of the world' feeling. They are open, fearless, more capable of withstanding opposition and generally very self-assured. 'Take me as you find me' should be their motto. Strong opinion, less fearful, more likely to be direct and straightforward.

The Second House, House of Money, Material Possessions and Self-Worth

I confess I do a lot of the wrong things: I smoke and I drink wine and people might be horrified at my eating habits – I eat when I'm hungry and if I'm not I don't.
Diana Rigg

This is the house that represents the things that we own. The practical world. Energy will be spent on accumulating possessions or financial security. Enjoyment will be found from holding, touching, truly experiencing things... tactile experiences like massage are generally treasured. All the senses need to be fulfilled and food is not a necessity, it can be a joy.

The Third House, House of Communication & Short Journeys

A word to the wise ain't necessary – it's the stupid ones that need the advice.
Bill Cosby

Like the third sign Gemini, the third house wants to engage with others by communicating with them. They would need a mobile phone, access to letters, telephones, conversations and all forms of communication. Being able to chat or write satisfies this house. As it also governs short journeys, having some means of transport is good.

The Fourth House, House of Home, Family & Roots

It's so obvious that animals have feelings and experience much the same emotions as we do. When you have a dog there is another heartbeat in the house. If you've been out and come home, there is an entirely different feeling to a house where there is dog waiting for you.
Jenny Seagrove

This is where the home becomes important. 'Family' in all its varied combinations will be a high priority. Cooking, snuggling up to others, pets, being close to significant others and the domestic world are all important. Children with this placement love to be home educated, but whatever they do stick the word 'home' in front of it and you'll succeed.

The Fifth House, House of Creativity & Romance

People are like stained-glass windows. They sparkle and shine when the sun is out, but when the darkness sets in, their true beauty is revealed only if there is a light from within.
Elisabeth Kübler-Ross

The fifth house is concerned with being able to shine. Being the centre of attention is also a plus. Red carpets, heaps of praise and appreciative recognition keep this combination happy. Creativity, drama, having lots of children or being with children, or creating or acting or being artistic are all expressed with the Sun here.

The Sixth House, House of Work & Health

I hated seeing myself on screen. I was full of complexes. I hated my face for a very, very long time.
Charlotte Gainsbourg

The sixth house has its focus on everything related to health. It also is the work that we do. The Cancer Sun here will want to be well, healthy and organised. It's not unheard of for them to work in the health and healing sector or at least be concerned about their own and others' health issues. Good at detail and intricate tasks.

The Seventh House, House of Relationships & Marriage

If you find someone you love in your life, then hang on to that love.
Princess Diana

The Cancer Sun here will want to share their life with a significant other. Being single won't wash. Until their close personal relationship is organised life feels bleak. When attached, life has new meaning. When they find their true love, their life seems complete and they can spread love and warmth around them.

The Eighth House, House of Life Force in Birth, Sex, Death & After-Life

Tell the truth. Sing with passion. Work with laughter. Love with heart. 'Cause that's all that matters in the end.
Kris Kristofferson

The intensity of the eighth house with the Cancer Sun makes an individual who is strong in character and un-swayed from their life's mission. Boredom is not on the menu! The ability to focus exclusively on one thing at a time can bring great results and if you add the word 'passion' in every now and then, they'll love you for it.

The Ninth House, House of Philosophy & Long Distance Travel

Being a rock star is like being a cult leader – you really have to be in your own religion.
Courtney Love

Provided that the ninth house Sun in Cancer can philosophise about life's true meaning all is well. Foreign countries, long journeys, and an interest in other cultures will be expressed here. Keep passports at the ready, this is the Sun placement that loves to travel. Spirituality is never far away in all its guises and they love to feel the world is there to explore.

The Tenth House, House of Social Identity & Career

I'm very interested in business astrology, and in mundane and financial astrology. But I'm more interested in people. If business astrology means dealing with people in companies, where I don't get to meet them – I'm just not interested.
Adrian Duncan

You would expect this individual to be focused on their career and how they feel others perceive them. Being able to be recognised in their chosen field, no matter how long this may take, will guide them to success. They will work long hours, and over many years to get to the highest level of their life that they can.

The Eleventh House, House of Social Life & Friendships

The unexpected connection with a stranger is often easier to make than one with people you know. It brings up the longing for connection we all feel.
Colin Hay

With the Cancer Sun in the 11th house individuals will want, no *need*: friends, groups, organizations, affiliations, societies that they can/will be members of. They don't see themselves in isolation to the world, they are part of it. Friendships are top of the list, so is charitable work and uniting the planet.

The Twelfth House, House of Spirituality

I was an observer. I liked to listen rather than openly express myself. This trait is something that I've retained over the years.
Giorgio Armani

I have noticed a lot of my clients who have Sun in the 12th really don't like living in the 'real world'. It all seems too painful and insensitive. The 12th house, like the sign Pisces, wants to merge with the fairies and angels and escape to Never-Never Land. They feel better when they have somewhere to escape to emotionally, be that the beach, on a hilltop, or in a nice warm bath every now and then.

Chapter Six

The Problems

As I've mentioned a few times before, clients don't come and see me when they've won the lottery. Most people make an appointment because something 'has happened'. These people need reassurance and lots of TLC so they can work their way out of whatever has gone wrong. Sometimes people come for a consultation because they're curious, but the majority of my clients have just had their world collapse and they want to know 'Why?'

Astrology is pretty good at explaining that 'why' and it also gives us a 'how long' answer too. If your husband has left you, your immediate thoughts are going to centre around 'How long will I be on my own?'... and similar worries.

If my client is a Cancer (or the other Water signs Scorpio and Pisces), it's very important that I find out how they feel.

With the Water signs most of the consultation will revolve around their *feelings* and it's only by talking about how they feel, how things happen, that makes them *feel* that way that they will they be better able to cope with whatever is happening.

I will need to know from the Air signs, Gemini, Libra and Aquarius, what they're thinking and the Fire signs Aries, Leo and Sagittarius what *actions* they want to take. What will they 'do'. And the Earth signs Taurus, Virgo and Capricorn, I will have to find out what practical plans they can put in place, what first steps they need to make to get to happiness.

Here are a few real things that happen in my practice and the sorts of solutions I will suggest.

My Cancer's Mother doesn't understand him/her

If I hear this statement, alarm bells start ringing. For a Cancer, mother is everything and if their relationship with her is bad, then their whole life feels like a struggle.

I do hear this quite a bit and it's very sad.

The sorts of things I suggest are easy and do-able. If your Cancer's mother doesn't understand him or her or has made their life unbearable by being cold or unfeeling or worse, don't despair.

First of all, get them to write Mum/Mom a letter. This isn't a letter that's actually going to be posted. Write the letter with as much feeling as possible (not hard for a Cancer). Put in there all the things that Mum didn't do, didn't say, how she made you feel weird for having feelings, how she didn't dry your eyes when you cried, how she didn't make you feel secure and snug and loved, and how all this made you feel. How she might have ignored you when you said you felt your feelings were hurt (another Cancer alarm bell), how she criticised or nagged or made nasty remarks. Write as much and for as long as you feel is right for you, then fold the letter into four, and safely burn it... and watch the flames engulf the words and the pain.

I suggest this a lot to my clients and it always has the desired effect that they feel lighter and less weighed down afterwards, as if years of pain and anger have been released. The people who 'say' it has had no effect are generally the ones who haven't actually done this exercise and have just thought about it. Thinking won't cure this. Solid action and real writing with a real pen on real paper is the only way. Don't do this on a computer either. Make it real. A computer doesn't have the same tactile experience as actual writing does and also doesn't tap into the part of the memory where all this hurt might be stored.

I feel suffocated by my Cancer's attention/love

Oh dear! You must be an Air sign (Aquarius/Gemini/Libra). As Cancer is such an emotionally in-tune sign, they can go overboard with their feelings which an Air sign can find difficult if they don't have any Water planets in their chart or planets in

Water houses (houses 4, 8 and 12).

There are a few ways you can help yourself. One of them is not to take your Cancer's feelings personally. They are feeling these feelings, not you. If you are getting bogged-down into them think of techniques that would suit you. Maybe you could carry a rose quartz crystal in your pocket and when it seems as if your Cancer is flooding you with emotional waves, you can stem the flow by imagining the crystal absorbing them and transmuting them into love and peace.

Of you could tell yourself they're not going to feel this way for long and like a wave the feelings will soon wash over and be gone.

Or you could have a little word with your Cancer and tell them you feel rather overwhelmed with their feelings, and agree on a workable solution to help things along. Don't make your Cancer feel any worse by blaming them for feeling this way. They don't have that same rational take on things you might have and will need acknowledgement and recognition of their hurts... and if you can give them a hug, they will soon recover their equilibrium and get back on course to 'normal' life.

My Cancer doesn't seem to want to leave home

The original working title of this book was 'How to Help a Cancer Leave Home' but I decided that I would use that as a difficulty within the book as being at home and leaving home are things that Cancers struggle with.

I shall explain.

Cancer, as we know, is ruled by the Moon, and the Moon in Western astrology is a nurturing and embracing influence. It's the thing that makes us feel snuggly, warm and loved. And the place where we mostly feel those emotions is at 'home' with Mum and Dad and our siblings. But, as you can appreciate, there is no such thing as a traditional home; as in reality, home is where the heart is, and that could be anywhere.

When a Cancer is growing up, they enjoy the whole being in-the-arms-of-the-ones-they-love or, equally, embracing-the-ones-they-love. It's a two-way street. Generally, and I say this cautiously, because there is always someone this won't apply to, Cancers love their mothers. They just do that automatically. As mother represents all those things they love: being cuddled, having tasty food, feeling together and feeling safe. Even if their relationships with their mothers are challenging, they still yearn for that one true love of mother-dom.

I can't tell you the amount of clients who have told me that one of their children just doesn't seem to want to leave home. And if I enquire a little further, their Sun sign is Cancer. The parents are generally Air or Fire signs, as they're the most independent signs... and there their child is, all grown-up, with a job and a car and a partner sometimes, and they still come home for dinner, still sleep in their bed in the childhood bedroom. They make themselves useful with helping around the house, doing shopping, paying bills, so any mother in her right mind surely wouldn't want them to fly the nest.

I even know a Cancer lady I read for who married a man, then divorced him and married his brother so she could continue to stay in the family home. The divorced brother even continued to live in the same house. We did some tie-cutting.

If you want your Cancer to leave home, you will have to plan very early in their life. Plan ahead. You might even have to downsize to help them leave, as even if you use their room for other purposes, they'll sleep on the sofa, or even on the floor. Make the moving out as gentle and as thought-out as you can. Encourage them to stay the night with friends. Explain you need your freedom too. Teach them about managing their finances and paying bills and all of the practical things that leaving home entails, otherwise you'll have them back in two months because they didn't pay the rent.

Find out what their Moon sign is, and work around satisfying that part of their psyche to make the move easier. If you're still having problems, get their full birth chart made up, and look at their 4th house and the planets that are in there (or not) as this will give you an idea of the type of home they feel most comfortable in and help them recreate it in their own home. Once a Cancer has made the move and created their 'own home' they're fine. It's just making that transition that can be more challenging.

Chapter Seven

The Solutions

I think by now we need to get a definition of what caring actually is, because before you can care for the Cancers you know, you need to understand exactly what caring is, and isn't.

I love the English language; it's so full of weird and wonderful differences. Some things seem perfectly straightforward, other things just don't make sense, but I think it's important to check what we're talking about when we say we must 'care for Cancers'.

My dictionary defines care as:

1. noun: Worry, anxiety; occasion for these; serious attention, caution (assembled with care, handle with care); protection, charge=*childcare*; thing to be done or seen to.
2. verb: Feel concern or interest (about, for); have liking for or wish to do (don't care for jazz, would you care to try?); provide for.
    Take care of: Look after, deal with.

If your Cancer is all upset about something, going 'there, there, oh dear' won't really work. You need to clearly assess their feelings, put them into perspective, acknowledge them, embrace them, give them space to exist but not at the expense of their sanity.

If your Cancer is so emotional that they're doing irrational things like spending lots of money they don't have, or have stopped eating or are talking about harming themselves, then get some professional help. Keeping in mind that most traditional medical Western approaches are with drugs. I would suggest counselling and certain alternative approaches first, provided the practitioner is licensed, experienced and insured to carry out that type of work... or at least use them in conjunction with the medical model.

The Dalai Lama says what helps us to a state of happiness from his book *The Art of Happiness: A Handbook for Living* is being gentle:

Our physical structure seems to be more suited to feelings of love and compassion. We can see how a calm, affectionate, wholesome state of mind has beneficial effects on our health and physical well-being. Conversely, feelings of frustration, fear, agitation, and anger can be destructive to our health. We can also see that our emotional health is enhanced by feelings of affection. To understand this, we need only to reflect on how we feel when others show us warmth and affection. Or, observe how our own affectionate feelings or attitudes automatically and naturally affect us from within, how they make us feel. These gentler emotions and the positive behaviours that go with them lead to a happier family and community life. So, I think that we can infer that our fundamental human nature is one of gentleness. And if this is the case, then it makes all the more sense to try to live a way of life that is more in accordance with this basic gentle nature of our being.

I agree with this type of thinking.

He explains further:

"I believe that the basic or underlying nature of human beings is gentleness."

How true!

And if your Cancer is an emotional wobbly mess, then *being gentle* needs to be your first thought and action. Surely if we were as a race to get our emotions into check, then there would be less war, frustration and unhappiness? This is where astrology is terribly useful and the flower essences I mentioned in Chapter Four will help. Once emotions are cared-for, we feel cared-for and wellness resumes.

If you're an Air sign, Aquarius Eckhart Tolle talks about this a lot in his *The Power of Now* and calls emotions "the pain body" and likens them to separate entities that invade our subconscious and cause us grief. I highly recommend his book if you're struggling with happiness, and the Dalai Lama's too.

I don't need to point out that turning to stimulants or alcohol will only make things worse. As Cancer Beatle Ringo Starr quite rightly pointed out:

That's all drugs and alcohol do, they cut off your emotions in the end.

Your approach to helping your emotional-meltdown Cancer will need a few tweaks depending on what type of Cancer they are. I've divided the suggestions into Ascendants and Moon signs so find the one that matches your Cancer's chart and use the suggestions to help both you and them cope. Remember the relevant flower essences too, as they work a treat in emotional situations. And may I just make a small request? Men have emotions too, so the suggestions in this book apply to men just as much as to women.

Aries Asc or Moon

Do something physical with your Cancer. Take them out of the house, somewhere where they can bash a ball, or run around, or get those feelings out of their system without bopping you on the head. A round of golf, a tennis match, a few hours swimming, a game of squash, rounders, basketball... something competitive but nothing that is going to get you in the firing line so don't go shooting... Aries is all about the body and energy, so something energetic is best. They can then thrash out their feelings on the green, court or pool and you can 'be' there for them while that happens.

Taurus Asc or Moon

Get the kettle on and some nice, low fat cakes, pastry or salad organised. Or go one better and take your Taurus/Cancer out for a nice meal. Somewhere beautiful with pretty surroundings, where the wallpaper matches the tablecloths, or the staff wear clean, smart uniforms. Don't even think about getting a takeaway or going to McD's; that won't work while they're in this mindset. Take things slowly, don't rush, and let them talk, or not.

Gemini Asc or Moon

You will need some form of transport to make a Gemini/Cancer combo feel better. It's a fact that they feel better making some sort of short journey, some change of scene, so get them into the car and let them talk, talk, talk… until they haven't got anything left to say about the problem. When they start commenting on passers-by or the scenery, you know they're feeling a little better.

Cancer Asc or Moon

Invite your double Cancer over for a home-cooked meal that you loving prepared yourself. It doesn't have to be cordon bleu, but it does have to be made with love by your own hands. Ignore any comments about how they might have done a better job themselves. This is just the grumpy bit getting an airing; so hold your tongue and let them relax into enjoying your company, and being with someone who cares. If there are any small animals around, or little children they can fuss over, they will feel better.

Leo Asc or Moon

You're going to have to work a little harder to please a Cancer who has Leo bits. Second best won't do. They want to feel exclusive attention from you and need a chance to let off steam.

You can volunteer to help. 'What shall I do' will go down well, but you might just find that they've got the solutions; they just want to act out how they feel about them. Prepare for major dramatics; this is a combination less likely to suffer quietly.

Virgo Asc or Moon

A wobbly Virgo/Cancer needs quiet space and cool, calm surroundings. They will be worrying about their health, so any advice that Deepak Chopra suggests will be helpful such as taking responsibility for feelings, feeling where they are in the body and what those sensations feel like, writing them down, releasing them with a ritual then celebrating their release. Thinking less always helps as all the Air signs think far too much, and do use Bach Flower Essence Centaury; it's a lifesaver for out-of-control worries.

Libra Asc or Moon

Be nice! Libra/Cancer will be an indecisive wreck and pointing that out won't help. Stay away from any decisions, don't ask them what they want; in troubled times they can barely think, so make all the decisions about lunch, shopping, cooking and eating. Find something truly beautiful and share it with them. Point out some lovely things that are true, take them to see a beautiful sunset, take a walk through a pretty meadow or landscaped garden. If you don't have the time or the money, set their computer to have a picture of nature on their screen saver. Listen to gentle music together. Just 'be'.

Scorpio Asc or Moon

You will need to be firm and centred with a Scorp/Cancer. Being fluffy and soft won't work. If you think of colours like deep blood red and things like being stung by a Scorpion you'll get the idea. They want to take drastic measures to make themselves feel better. This can involve throwing caution to the winds and doing something completely out of character, so I tend to suggest to Scorp/Cancer clients to do things like write a letter to the people or problem concerned... and burn it... and watch the flames eat away the problem. Provided the intention is deep and meaningful it will work just as well as drastic actions that will be later regretted.

Sagittarius Asc or Moon

As a Fire sign, the Sag/Cancer will want to let off steam in an active, physical way. As they so love long distance travel and philosophical pursuits, a quick trip away to a distant, exotic country works well, as does finding the 'meaning' to what is going on. Prepare to quote philosophical texts such as the Bible or other spiritual works and immerse them in the 'bigger picture'. They won't want to think about teeny, unimportant things during a personal crisis, so don't remind them of petty things. Stay big.

Capricorn Asc or Moon

As this is a more serious combination, your Cap/Cancer will enjoy wise words from an elder, someone older than them, who has been there, done that very thing they're fretting about, and has got the tee shirt. They like to think of serious, practical, traditional subjects that have meaning; and when they're in a head-spin, prefer and respond better to wise council. If you've got any elderly relatives, drag your Cap/Cancer to see them, so they can understand that everything-will-be-alright. To get to be old, you have to have taken some risks, so finding out how this older relative might have survived their own tragedies will inspire your Cancer to better things. If not, tell them about how your mother/grandfather/elderly neighbour handled it, or how someone from long ago that you heard of/read about did it. Use examples that contain results and feelings.

Aquarius Asc or Moon

Anyone with Aquarius planets loves to do something weird and wacky every now and then. They won't follow the 'normal' life path and prefer to almost be the outsider, so if their life goes wobbly, don't expect to get them back on track with 'normal' solutions. One thing is for sure, they will want their friends to stand by them, and will enjoy the support of organisations or clubs or groups that they have an affinity for. In the short term, getting outside in the fresh air helps, as Aquarius is an Air sign, so deep breathing and meditation also help.

Pisces Asc or Moon

The sign of the mystical and spiritual Pisces/Cancer will love the more esoteric solutions to problems so you can use Angel cards and the flower essences to assist. They also need time and space to reconfigure, as they're more likely to have picked-up everyone else's feelings and angst which might have contributed to present problems. Keeping a dream diary also helps during wobbly phases.

Chapter Eight

Caring Tactics

OK. Now you know quite a bit about Cancer the sign, the Moon and the important bits of a birth chart. We'll now discuss the various different Cancers you'll come across in real life and how the sign fares in each setting. We've talked a lot about mothers and mothering but obviously not every Cancer is female. I know plenty of Cancer men who are fathers and they don't mother their children but they do do the nurturing and caring thing with them. Some are even perfectly happy being stay-at-home dads, something that should be encouraged. There is no reason in this modern age where men can marry men, why men cannot also look after their children. It doesn't revolve around being male or female, but does need to involve a caring nature and an ability to multitask. Ask any parent who's had to make a meal, answer the phone, keep a toddler from crawling up or down the stairs and answer questions from an enquiring older sibling.

Your Cancer Child

Hugs can do great amounts of good – especially for children.
Princess Diana

Your Cancer child will be a little bundle of joy when born. The Homeopathic remedy constitutional-type Calc Carb is very Cancer-like. They enjoy tactile contact, don't like too much change, will sit and wonder at things and smile and gurgle when cuddled. To make your Cancer baby feel at home, all you have to do is unleash your inner, caring mother-self and everything else will fall into place.

Joanne is a businesswoman and runs her own company. She

told me what it was like to *be* a Cancer child. For your Cancer baby to feel content, you need to *always* take their feelings into account. She tells us about how her mother coped with her moods:

I would get really upset and in a mood, because I thought I wasn't being heard, then she'd put me upstairs in my room and tell me to stay in there and what would happen is I'd get really upset because I'd been isolated... and I'd not been nurtured. Then I'd get even more into my emotion. I remember really crying, and being really upset and taking that to an extreme and I was left to diffuse it myself, which took a really long time, whereas at any point if someone had come into the room and said, "Hey, come on, what's happening, tell me about it, let's chat about it"...or "I've got this for you, or here's some food or a flannel to wipe your face" or whatever, something nurturing, something gentle, that would have been fine.

It's no good ignoring your Cancer child's feelings. Joanne elaborates:

Being given the space to talk about our emotions, and in the talking about them, we might feel it's a storm in a teacup.

When they're old enough to want to talk about how they feel, doing the room-putting-in-thing won't help, in fact it makes matters worse. I sometimes feel that people who don't want to hear someone else's feelings generally aren't in touch with their own feelings, but don't take that as totally true. It's just a feeling.

Some mothers deal with their Cancer children in rather extreme ways. Richard Branson tells us how his mother used a rather drastic tactic:

My mother was determined to make us independent. When I was four years old, she stopped the car a few miles from our house and made me find my own way home across the fields. I got hopelessly lost.

Maureen is an Aries housewife and small business owner with a Cancer teen son. She lives and works in Brighton, UK. Luke is a Cancer with Sun in the 11th, with Virgo Ascendant and Moon in Aries:

Always been strong and silent. Very sensitive and rarely shows it, just looks 'startled' but is always spot on when he does say what mood he thinks people are in and what their thoughts of him are.

Wants everyone to be happy as a group and to work as a team.

Wants a harmonious life.

Expresses himself through his art – painting Warhammer and drawing sci-fi characters.

Likes being with a group of friends and is happy on his own at home.

Happy to be himself and if people don't like him for who he is that's fine.

He'll stand in front of a friend to defend him and will take the blame to diffuse a situation.

If we were to analyse his chart, we'd say the friendship thing is Sun in the 11th, the Virgo Ascendant likes the detailed drawing thing and the other attributes are definitely Cancer-type, especially the knowing about other people's moods.

I'm not suggesting that you pussyfoot around your Cancer child and imagine that everything and anything is going to affect them, but keep in mind that it helps if you take into account their feelings about things.

It's no good asking 'What do you *think* about this or that'; you'd be better off asking 'How do you *feel*' about the subject in hand. Also it certainly helps if you find out what learning style they have and adapt accordingly.

They may be kinaesthetic, visual or aural, and so you should communicate so they understand you.

A kinaesthetic child will need to physically feel things to understand them and will learn by touching, holding, doing things. My Libra son is kinaesthetic and it's no good showing him how to do something; he has to 'do' it himself, has to actually experience something to understand it. If I need him to understand what I'm telling him, a small touch on his arm does the trick. If your kinaesthetic child won't put their shoes on, shouting, telling, yelling just won't sink in, you have to make a gentle touch and give simple, short sentence instructions.

A visual learning style child likes to look to understand. They will gaze into your eyes as you speak, will want you to look at them when they're talking. Show them what you mean; it's easier for them to understand. I'm visual and feel I'm not being heard if someone talks to me and they're looking at their feet, and I felt this way for years until I found out these learning styles. I can also look at something and copy it, and understand it, which might be why I love astrology so much as I spend all day looking at charts!!

An aural learner child will understand things from hearing them. Will imitate your words, make sounds, need to hear things to understand them, might be good at music or singing because they remember sounds better. With these children it's best to make sure your voice is clear and instructions are equally clear, and you can get them interested in things by making them into songs or poems or nursery rhymes.

It does help if you find your own learning style first, otherwise you'll only see the world through your own viewpoint (that was said like a visual person!).

Your Cancer Boss

You might not know that your boss is a Cancer, especially if they're male... until someone in their family is ill or there is a big celebration like a wedding anniversary, or their mother reaches an old-age milestone, then their true colours will come out.

In a YouGov survey conducted in September 2012, 2010 people were asked about their views of their managers.

The findings paint a positive picture of managers in the UK, who don't micromanage, with 47% of respondents saying they are given the freedom to get on with their work uninterrupted. They also make their workers feel comfortable (47%), give proper constructive criticism (36%) and are calm under pressure (33%).

Ultimately, workers want a manager who is fair (30%), relaxed (20%) and inspirational (19%), with Sir Richard Branson topping the poll (26%) for the famous person that workers would choose as a manager based on his management style.

This is very interesting because Richard is a Cancer and what qualities were most enjoyed by employees? Someone who *'made them feel comfortable'*. I had to chuckle when I read this as it seemed to so describe the ultimate Cancer boss.

Richard has a Leo Ascendant, so he doesn't mind being in the spotlight, but his Sun is in the 12th, so he prefers to lead from the back, which is a bit of a dilemma for Cancers who have Leo Ascendants. One part of them wants to be on display and the other part wants to hide away. Mr Branson also has Moon in Virgo, so his management style will mean he's included all those small details that his employees will enjoy.

Now your boss might not be anything like Richard Branson and might have all the negative qualities of the Cancer Sun by being moody, snappy and evasive. To make your working life more bearable, it will help if you find out all about your boss' family and include mention of them as and when you can. If your boss is female, a few words about their nearest and dearest every now and then will score you high points. Obviously none of this will work if you're not sincere, as your average Water sign will spot at 50 paces someone who is just buttering them up.

A good Cancer boss will want to make you 'part of the family' and will gladly employ other relatives of yours provided they stay true to the company's mottos.

Your Cancer (female) Lover

To successfully date a Cancer lady, you will have to be practical, earth centred, and good at cuddles. You won't have to be brainy or top-of-the-class or own a large car or act important. You will need to be emotionally honest and reasonably hard working.

Here we have Zara who lives in London, is in her late 20s and is looking for a partner:

> *I enjoy swimming and cycling more than any other sport, used to be a member of school swim team and will only go to the gym for a spinning session. I feel more comfortable in guys' company and enjoy a little chat about sports/technology/politics a lot more than girls' ramble about their beauty rituals... I am absolutely addicted to chocolate, fashion/interior design blogs, Skype and music. I enjoy early yet lazy mornings with endless green tea top-ups; long relaxing showers – never hot baths; love to read, watch, listen, taste, laugh, feel, discover, learn, analyse, understand and... disagree. Always have my opinion, although I often prefer to keep it to myself or at least I am careful as to who I share it with. Since I like to observe and contemplate, I tend to read people well. I may not be an open book or wear my heart on my sleeve, but finding a key to open me up is definitely not mission impossible.*

She says she is looking for someone who is:

> *fun to be around, ambitious, with lots of energy, passion for life and knowledge, intelligent and observant, witty and sharp, resourceful and reliable, sweet and caring, a family guy with tons of patience and... beautiful eyes!*

Your Cancer lover will not need flashy displays of affection or expensive dates, but if you remember the name of her dog/cat/fluffy-pet/best friend/favourite anything you will do well. She won't want you to tattoo her name on your arm but will love it if you walk together, in moonlight on a secluded beach, and you write her name in the sand.

If she gets on well with her family, you will become part of that tribe too. If you give her mother trips to the shops, or help with decorating the house, or can rewire a plug or anything remotely handy and domestic, you'll also appeal to her inner desires.

Make sure you find out early in the relationship if she wants children. It's no good leaving it until you've been dating for a number of years, then to expect her to change whichever way she's made up her mind. That will be one thing she's sure about. She either will, or she won't. And if she doesn't want to actually become a mother herself, you can be sure she'll want a pet or some other living being that she can shower with affection.

Your Cancer (male) Lover

Harry is a truck driver and lives and works in Texas. He tells us what he likes, what makes him happy:

Fishing, dancing, playing softball, singing in the choir, our house, cooking, my partner.

As I have said many times, if you want to get along with someone who is a different Sun sign from you, you need to understand life from his or her point of view.

If you're a go-getting Sagittarius, hanging around with a home-loving Cancer might be fun for all of 5 minutes, then you're going to get itchy feet and want out.

Generally speaking people get along better with other people who are either the same element as them or one that is complementary. I know the astrological reason why, but I can't give you any science or evidence I'm afraid.

Sam is in his 40s and looking for a partner. He tells us a little about himself:

Thoughtful, creative, youthful (hanging in there!). Cancerian origi-nally trained in science but now working as a self-employed person. I design, make and sell ceramics and spend a lot of time in the countryside or on the sea (I like boats). I really enjoy being out and about either alone or with company, but I'm not the sort of person that needs a lot of people around me to feel alive.

He then tells us about what he likes:

Although active, I'm not an activity freak, and like to spend as much time 'being' as doing. Nature is the best balm of all. I'm now based in Gloucestershire but have lived/worked in London in the past and still visit there regularly. On balance though, give me the country and coast any day.

I guess I'm quite practical and apart from making things, I can also mend them (and sometimes mess them up as well… mmm). I also like books, handmade stuff, growing some veg and people with style and manners. I don't do negative waves, and prefer to look on the brighter side of life. I try to do some meditation every day if I can. Easy-going, open-minded and ready for the right woman. Where are they?

I loved the way he said he liked making and mending things and 'handmade' things. If you ever really want to touch a Cancer's heart, give them a present you have made yourself, especially for them, and you'll have them won-over.

Your male Cancer will prefer you to be gentle and gracious if you can. Failing that he'll prefer you to keep your more angry feelings to yourself and not overwhelm him with negative or hurtful emotions. I once read: find out how a man treats his mother, because this will be how he treats you in old age. I don't know where I read it or when, but in my world it certainly holds true. Someone who treats their mother well will also treat you well when the kids are grown and you're in your rocking chair.

Find out as soon as you can what Moon sign your Cancer male lover has, as that will be the way to his heart. Is it in Taurus, enjoying good food, stable finances and earthy sex, or is it in Sagittarius wanting to explore the world or at least the spiritual part of life? Keeping those two things in mind will help you more than you realize as your dating progresses.

Make sure you meet the family as soon as you can too, because it will be a case of 'love me, love my family'... and the better you all get along, the lighter your load will be.

What to do if your Cancer relationship ends

Fire sign
If you are a Fire sign: Aries, Leo or Sagittarius, you will need something active and exciting to help you get over your relationship ending. You will also need to use the element of Fire in your healing process.

Get a nice nightlight candle and light it and recite:

I... (your name) do let you... (Cancer's name) go, in the freedom and with love so that I am free to attract my true soul-love.

Leave the nightlight in a safe place to completely burn away. Allow at least an hour. In the meantime gather up any belongings or possessions that are your (now) ex-lover's and deliver them back to your Cancer. It's polite to telephone first and notify your ex when you will be arriving.

If you have any photos of you together or other mementos or even gifts, don't be in a rush to destroy them, as some Fire signs are prone to do. Better to put them away in a box in the attic or garage until you feel a little less upset.

In a few months' time go through the box and keep the things you like and give away the things you don't.

Earth sign

If you are an Earth sign: Taurus or Virgo or Capricorn, you will feel less inclined to do something dramatic or outrageous. It might also take you slightly longer to recover your equilibrium, so allow yourself a few weeks and a maximum of three months to grieve.

You will be using the Earth element to help your healing which can be expressed by using crystals.

The best crystals to use are the ones associated with your Sun sign and also with protection.

Taurus = Emerald
Virgo = Agate
Capricorn = Onyx

Cleanse your crystal in fresh running water. Wrap it in some pretty silk fabric, and then go on a walk into the countryside. When you find a suitable spot, that is quiet and where you won't be disturbed, dig a small hole and place your crystal in the ground.

Spend a few minutes thinking about your relationship, the good times and the bad. Forgive yourself for any mistakes you may have made.

Imagine a beautiful plant growing from the ground where you have buried your crystal, and the plant blossoming and growing strong.

This will represent your new love that will be with you when the time is right.

Air sign

If you're an Air sign: Gemini, Libra or Aquarius, you might want to talk about what happened first before you finish the relationship. Air signs need reasons and answers, and can waste precious life-energy looking for those answers. You might need to meet with your Cancer to tell him/her exactly what you think/thought about his/her opinions, ideas and thoughts. You might also be tempted to tell him/her what you think about them now, which I do *not* recommend.

Far better to put those thoughts into a tangible form by writing your ex-Cancer a letter. It is not a letter that you are actually going to post, but you are going to put as much energy into writing it *as if* you were actually going to send it.

Write to them thus:

Dear Cancer,
I expect you will be happy now in your new life, but there are a few things I would like to know and understand before I say goodbye.

Then list all the annoying habits that your (now) ex-Cancer indulged in. Make a list as long as you like. Put in as much detail as you feel comfortable with, including things like how many times they wept on your shoulder but didn't help you when you got into a tangle at work, or didn't want to watch the same TV programmes as you. Keep writing until you can write no more, then end your letter with something similar:

Even though we were obviously not suited, and I suffered because of this, I wish you well on your path.

Or some other positive comment.

Then tear your letter into teeny little pieces and put them into a small container. We are now going to use the element of Air to rectify the situation.

Take a trip to somewhere windy and high, like the top of a hill, and when you're ready, open your container and sprinkle a *few* random pieces of your letter into the wind. Don't use the entire letter or you run the risk of littering, just enough pieces to be significant. Watch those little pieces of paper fly into the distance and imagine them connecting with the nature spirits.

Your relationship has now ended.

Water sign

If you are a Water sign: our friend Cancer, Scorpio or Pisces, you might find it more difficult to recover quickly from your relationship. You might find yourself weeping at inopportune moments, or when you hear 'your' song on the radio, or when you see other couples happily being in each other's company. You might lie awake at night worrying that you have ruined your life and your ex-Cancer is having all the fun. As you might have gathered by now, this is unlikely. Your ex might be as upset as you.

Your emotional healing therefore needs to incorporate the Water element.

As you are capable of Weeping for the World, the next time you are in floods of tears capture one small teardrop and place it into a small glass. Have one handy just for this purpose. Decorate it if you feel like it. Small flowers, stars, or twinkly things.

Now fill your glass to the top with tap water and place it on a table then recite the following:

This loving relationship with you… (Cancer's name) has ended.
I reach out across time and space to you.
My tears will wash away the hurt I feel.
I release you from my heart, mind and soul.
We part in peace.

And then slowly drink the water. Imagine your hurt dissolving away, freeing you from all anxieties and releasing you from sadness. Then spend the next few weeks being nice to yourself. If you need to talk, find someone you trust and confide in them. Keep tissues handy.

Your Cancer Friend

We can live without religion and meditation, but we cannot survive without human affection.
Dalai Lama

Most people enjoy friendships and Cancers are no different. Jofrina comes from Eastern Europe and is studying creative writing at university in the UK. For a long time she had singing lessons and had this to say about her Cancer teacher:

They're very perceptive of other people's feelings; they often know just the right thing to say. My singing teacher could be a good counsellor, I think... He once told me that some students sometimes come over just to talk, even after they've quit the learning. I myself haven't had lessons for almost two years, but I go to see him occasionally, because I feel he can understand me very well and just say those right things I need to hear. Definitely the person who can provide both comfort and guidance. When I first started his lessons, after a few months everyone started asking how is it, and one thing that I told everyone (and it's true) was, "I finish the lesson, close the door on my way out and I feel that I want to live." That's my deepest impression of my experience with him.

Here we have the Cancer ability to make someone want to be with them, because of their deep understanding of the human psyche. If you're an Air or Fire sign, don't spend too much time with your Cancer friend as their emotional way of living will tire you and you'll only bicker or argue. Best to see them regularly but not frequently. Obviously, if you've got compatible charts, then see them as much as you like. Water and Earth signs get on better as friends with Cancers as they can empathise with their emotions and offer help when they hit a wobbly patch. If you get on well, you'll find after a while that you become 'extended family' and will be invited to weddings, christenings, funerals and family gatherings. Be respectful of this inclusion as it means they really value your friendship. If you want to ever give them a gift, something you've made yourself will send them into raptures. I have a lovely Cancer friend who knits homemade wonderfully comfortable socks. If my feet are feeling tired or cold in the winter, her lovely socks make my feet feel wonderful!

Your Cancer Mother

I want them to have an understanding of people's emotions, people's insecurities, people's distress and people's hopes and dreams.
Princess Diana

Having a Cancer mother is either a blessing or a curse. It all depends on what Sun sign you are, and your own Moon sign. If you're the Airy sort, full of ideas, wanting change, prepared to move house every five minutes, having a Cancer mother might prove problematic.

One thing is for sure, she will love you, regardless. When you're small, she'll also find it hard to criticize you and will see your first steps and early learning as wonderful events. You (hopefully) will be the recipient of oodles of love and care.

Prince William is a Cancer with Sagittarius Ascendant, Sun in the 7th and Moon in Cancer too. His mother Princess Diana also had a Sagittarius Ascendant, Sun in the 7th and Moon in Aquarius. If you live in the UK or have ever watched the news, you will know how much Prince William valued his mother, and still does. He even gave his future wife his mother's own engagement ring… As William and Diana's charts are so similar, with the same Sun sign and house placement, it's hardly surprising that William is so devoted and dedicated to her memory and his loss was so great. Any interviewer who asks him about his mother will not hear him say anything negative about her, which is lovely.

Problems arise if you move away from your Cancer mother or don't stay in contact when you do move away. Then your Cancer mother will fade away into unhappiness.

Grant is a fun-loving, adventurous Sagittarius, with a look-at-me Leo Ascendant. The Fire signs don't have much patience and want things as soon as possible. He found his Cancer mother a restraining influence:

> *So, Leo Asc loves the sun. Sag Sun loves the outdoors. I almost got a horse when I was a kid but my Cancer mother was worried that I would kill myself. I was notorious for falling out of trees. I used to love to climb trees. I still do!!! Hehehehe.*

I suppose the worst time to have a Cancer mother is when you hit your teens. There you are all fired-up with hormones, wanting to be out every night, not coming home for tea or dinner and being self-sufficient and independent. This might be when problems occur. Talking it out with your mother would be best, so she doesn't go into a depression because her 'baby' is leaving home. Again, any gift you ever make will sit on the mantelpiece as a treasured possession. Make things easier for your Cancer mother when you do leave home. Maybe you could make a treasure box for her containing pictures and items from your childhood to remind her you're still around. And do phone home regularly. She's genuinely interested in your well-being.

Sheila Munro is one of the daughters of Cancer novelist Alice Munro.

My mother has always talked about wanting to be the opposite kind of mother from her own mother, whom she saw as moralistic, demanding, smothering, and emotionally manipulative.

However, Alice's plan to not be "smothering" only resulted in her distancing herself from her children. In her book *Lives of Mothers & Daughters* Sheila describes how she thought her Cancer mother wrote about them and their family in her novels even going as far as to say:

She was like the young mother in [the well-known Alice Munro story] *"Miles City, Montana", who sees herself as a detached observer.*

Sheila doesn't criticise her mother in her book, but she does explain how difficult it is to be mothered by someone whose mind is on something else.

Now, your Cancer mother might not be famous like Diana or Alice, good thing too, and hopefully will enjoy parenting you. If she doesn't, check to see what sign her Moon is in, and help her to satisfy that part of her chart. You'll be glad you did when you see the transformation. For a Cancer to have their Moon sign acknowledged is a short cut to true happiness.

Your Cancer Dad

Fatherhood is pretending the present you love most is soap-on-a-rope.
Bill Cosby

Your Cancer father will probably be a good cook, or at least be able to rustle up a meal. He'll enjoy watching you grow. Where you might fall out is if you don't want to join him in the family business. Some Cancer dads that I know run a business and would love their children to take over from them when they get too old to work or they retire. I expect a lot of those old 'Smith... and Son' businesses were started by Cancers. Keeping it in the family is always a priority.

But like with everything astrological, it does depend on what sign you are, and what Moon sign your dad has.

You might find that if your dad has his Sun in the first house, or he has an Aries Moon, that he's into sports or physical things, while if he has Sun in the 12th or 4th, or Moon in Pisces, he's a bit softer and more emotional.

My advice would be to get your own chart sorted out first and an understanding of your own needs, before you look at your dad's chart and get critical. I've had students that did their family horoscopes and were amazed and found 'things fell into place' about their parents. It does help with understanding someone.

As a general rule, your Cancer dad will be emotionally supportive and will be fine about things like nappies and babies and will enjoy being a parent. He will also be as concerned about money as a Taurus and, for a Cancer, money represents security and safety... something they constantly strive for.

Marion is an Aries, married to Tom; we met him earlier. They have two daughters.

He is a very hard worker taking care of all of the grocery shopping, vacuuming, scrubbing, repairs, cars, money (keeps meticulous records and I must report everything I spend). I clean up after him in the kitchen, clean the bathrooms, do the yard work, the thinking, the social stuff.

She also tells us:

I might add, he is hard to know, refusing to give any opinions on controversial matters. He's VERY uncomfortable when people disagree, even an exchange of differing opinions among friends. It's hard to solve problems as he cannot take criticism (or even suggestions), however mild. He seemed to think he had to be perfect, but I think he has gotten past that. He does not have great social skills, which I've attributed to being an only child. His only topics of conversation are food, sports, weather and the price of gas.

He also told us what was the most memorable event in his life:

Navy. Seeing the aircraft carrier for the first time. It was so damn big. All the people I got to know. Saw 30 countries. I grew up in the Navy gaining 6 inches and 35 pounds. Stopped being a picky eater.

Marion tells us:

He went into the Navy out of high school. He was a communication technician and was good at what he did.

Notice there is nothing weird, way-out or wacky about a Cancer father. Nothing that stands out more than those things we could all do with more of: caring, consideration and consistency.

Aquarius Charlotte's father was a Cancer and I asked her how emotional she thought he was. Here is her reply:

I'll use a scale of 1–10, with 10 being the most emotional: Dad was 8.

Have I seen him cry? Yes and that was when my mother died, and it was only a little, being suppressed. A few years later when his cat died, though, he wrote to me and admitted that his eyes had been even more irrigated after the cat's death than they were when his wife died. (I told him I believe that's common, largely because the grief over a pet's death is usually not shared, but borne alone by the owner.)

Your Cancer Sibling

To get on well with your Cancer sibling, again you need to keep in mind not only their Moon sign but your signs as well. If your Moons get on, you'll find that will reduce a whole load of anguish.

Here is a young teen Sagittarius girl who has fallen out with her sister:

She's too sensitive. She gets upset over the tiniest things then gets an attitude, which is annoying. She tries to put people in check and she doesn't even have all of her facts. She likes to look like some kind of innocent nurturing victim who just tries to help people and she's not.

This young lady obviously knows about Cancer's key characteristics, but she finds her sister overuses them. As Sagittarius is so motivated by freedom, having a sister who is Cancer and loves the home and Mom, and home cooking and snuggly things will seem like a complete contrast to her own needs of freedom, travel, the eternal quest for 'answers to life, the universe... and everything'... and less likely to bring understanding. Her sister might never leave home and might care for their parents when they're elderly, while she will be travelling the world and contemplating life's Big Questions.

I hope you have enjoyed reading about *How to Care for a Cancer* and have learned a little about Astrology and how it can help you understand someone.

If we all understood each other, maybe we'd get along better.

I wish you all the peace in the world.

References

1. http://cdn.yougov.com/today_uk_import/YG-Archives-Life-YouGov-Horoscope-121010.pdf

2. *The Astrologers and Their Creed*, Christopher McIntosh, 1971, Arrow Books Ltd, imprint of the Hutchinson Group, London

3. *Essentials Astronomy: A Beginner's Guide to the Sky at Night*, Paul Sutherland, 2007, Igloo Books Ltd
The Astronomy Handbook: Guide to the Night Sky, Clare Gibson, Kerswell Books Ltd

4. *Return to the Moon: Exploration, Enterprise, and Energy in the Human Settlement of Space*, Harrison Schmitt, 2006, Springer Publishing Company, New York, NY 10036

5. http://www.guardian.co.uk/theguardian/2007/oct/20/weekend7.weekend3

6. *The New Waite's Compendium of Natal Astrology*, Colin Evans, edited by Brian EF Gardener, 1967, Routledge and Kegan Paul Ltd, London, UK

7. http://www.world-of-wisdom.com/02_software/interpreter.htm

8. *Astrology for Dummies*, Rae Orion, 1999, IDG Books Worldwide, Inc., Foster City, CA 94404

9. *Linda Goodman's Sun Signs*, Linda Goodman, 1976, Pan Books Ltd, London SW10

10. *The Instant Astrologer*, Felix Lyle and Bryan Aspland, 1998,

Piatkus Books, London W1

11. http://skywriter.wordpress.com/2011/07/29/your-interview-questions-for-donna-part-2/

The Moon in Your Life: Being a Lunar Type in a Solar World, Donna Cunningham, 1996, Weiser Books

The Art of Happiness: A Handbook for Living, HH Dalai Lama and Howard C. Cutler, MD, 1998, Hodder and Stoughton, Euston Road, London

YouGov survey Reed employment http://tiny.cc/isztkw

Lives of Mothers & Daughters: Growing Up with Alice Munro, Sheila Munro, 2002, McClelland & Stewart, Ltd.

Further Information

The Astrological Association
www.astrologicalassociation.com

The Bach Centre, the Dr Edward Bach Centre, Mount Vernon, Bakers Lane, Brightwell-cum-Sotwell, Oxon, OX10 0PZ, UK www.bachcentre.com

Natural Friends ethical dating site www.natural-friends.com

Astrological Chart Information

Chart information and birth data from astro-databank at www.astro.com and www.astrotheme.com.

No accurate birth data

Aimée Ann Duffy, 25th June 1984, Bangor, Gwynedd, Wales, Sun Cancer, Moon Aries

Franz Kafka, 3rd July 1883, Prague, Czech Republic, Sun Cancer, Moon Gemini

Tom Cruise, 3rd July 1962, Syracuse, New York, USA, Sun Cancer, Moon Leo

Kristen Anne Bell, 18th July 1980, Huntington Woods, Michigan, USA, Sun Cancer, Moon Libra

Nelson Mandela, 18th July 1918, Umtata, SAFR, (poss 2.54pm), Sagittarius Ascendant, Sun in 8th, Moon Scorpio

Cyndi Lauper, 22nd June 1953, Queens, New York, USA, Sun Cancer, Moon Scorpio

Ascendant

Bill Cosby, 12th July 1937, Philadelphia, PA, USA, 00.30am, Aries Ascendant, Sun in 3rd, Moon Virgo

Gerald Rudolph Ford, 14th July 1913, Omaha, NE, USA, 0.43am, Taurus Ascendant, Sun in 3rd, Moon Sagittarius

Alan Turing, 23rd June 1912, London, England, UK, 2.15am, Gemini Ascendant, Sun in 1st, Moon Libra

Brigitte Nielsen, 15th July 1963, Copenhagen, Denmark, 6.20am, Leo Ascendant, Sun in 12th, Moon Taurus

Nancy Reagan (Anne Frances Robbins), 6th July 1921, Manhattan, NY, 1.18pm, Libra Ascendant, Sun in 9th, Moon Leo

Robin Williams, 21st July 1951, Chicago, IL, USA, 1.34pm, Scorpio Ascendant, Sun in 9th, Moon Pisces

Hermann Hesse, 2nd July 1887, Calw, Germany, 6.30pm,

Sagittarius Ascendant, Sun in 7th, Moon Pisces

Edmund Hillary, 20th July 1919, Papakura, New Zealand, 4pm, Capricorn Ascendant, Sun in 7th, Moon Aries

Emmeline Pankhurst, 14th July 1858, Manchester, England, UK, 9.30pm, Aquarius Ascendant, Sun in 6th, Moon Virgo

Elisabeth Kübler-Ross, 8th July 1926, Zurich, Switzerland, 10.45pm, Pisces Ascendant, Sun in 5th, Moon Cancer

Ringo Starr, 7th July 1940, Liverpool, England, UK, 0.05am, Pisces Ascendant, Sun in 4th, Moon Leo

Moon

Diana Rigg, 20th July 1938, Doncaster, England, UK, 2am, Gemini Ascendant, Sun in the 2nd, Moon Aries

Meryl Streep, 22nd June 1949, Summit, NJ, USA, 8.05am, Leo Ascendant, Sun in 11th, Moon Taurus

Courtney Love, 9th July 1964, San Francisco, CA, USA, 2.08pm, Libra Ascendant, Sun in 9th, Moon in Cancer

George Michael, 25th June 1963, Finchley, London, England, UK, 6am, Cancer Ascendant, Sun in 12th, Moon in Leo

Harrison Schmitt, 3rd July 1935, Santa Rita, NM, USA, 11.02pm, Pisces Ascendant, Sun in the 4th, Moon Leo

Willem Dafoe, 22nd July 1955, Appleton, WI, USA, 7.30pm, Aquarius Ascendant, Sun in 6th, Moon Virgo

Dalai Lama XIV, 6th July 1935, Tengster/Qinhai, China, 4.38am, Cancer Ascendant, Sun in 1st, Moon Virgo

Marc Almond, 9th July 1957, Southport, England, UK, 5am, Cancer Ascendant, Sun in 1st, Moon Sagittarius

Ernest Hemingway, 21st July 1899, Oak Park, Il, USA, 8am, Virgo Ascendant, Sun in 11th, Moon Capricorn

Shelley von Strunckel, 15th July 1946, Hollywood, CA, USA, 4.42pm, Sagittarius Ascendant, Sun in 8th, Moon Aquarius

Cat Stevens, 21st July 1948, London, England, UK, 12pm, Libra Ascendant, Sun in 10th, Moon Aquarius

Diana, Princess of Wales, 1st July 1961, Sandringham, England,

UK, 7.45pm, Sagittarius Ascendant, Sun in 7th, Moon Aquarius

Houses

Jenny Seagrove, 4th July 1958, Kuala Lumpur, Malaysia, 0.38am, Aries Ascendant, Sun in 4th, Moon Aquarius

Charlotte Gainsbourg, 21st July 1971, London, England, UK, 10pm, Aquarius Ascendant, Sun in 6th, Moon Cancer

Kris Kristofferson, 22nd June 1936, Brownsville, TX, USA, 3.30pm, Scorpio Ascendant, Sun in 8th, Moon Leo

Adrian Duncan, 17th July 1949, York, England, UK, 11.46am, Libra Ascendant, Sun in 10th, Moon Aries

Colin Hay, 29th June 1953, Kilwinning, Scotland, UK, 10.20am, Virgo Ascendant, Sun in 11th, Moon Aquarius

Giorgio Armani, 11th July 1934, Piacenza, Italy, 7.20am, Leo Ascendant, Sun in 12th, Moon Pisces

Other mentions

Alice Munro, 10th July 1931, Wingham, Canada, 9pm, Aquarius Ascendant, Sun in 6th, Moon Taurus

Dodona Books offers a broad spectrum of divination systems to suit all, including Astrology, Tarot, Runes, Ogham, Palmistry, Dream Interpretation, Scrying, Dowsing, I Ching, Numerology, Angels and Faeries, Tasseomancy and Introspection.

A light look at the Star Sign Cancer. Have you ever cared for a Cancer, literally or figuratively? Do you know why being caring is so important to them? Do you know why being able to express their emotions is so important to them?

This insider information will guide you through the process of easily making a natal chart using free on-line resources. You will discover how to find the three key points that will help you Care for a Cancer better. Drawing on her extensive client files and using real-life examples, Mary English gently guides you in learning "How To Care for a Cancer".

Mary English is a professional Astrologer who uses her skills in her private practice to empower her clients and guide them to a fuller life. She lives in Bath, England.

www.dodona-books.com

DODONA BOOKS

Body, Mind & Spirit
UK £7.99
US $11.95

US $11.95
ISBN 978-1-78279-063-1

Cover image © Shutterstock
Cover design by Design Deluxe

9 781782 790631